Nationalism and Political Identity

Nationalism and Political Identity

Sandra Fullerton Joireman

continuum
LONDON • NEW YORK

Continuum

The Tower Building
11 York Road
London, SE1 7NX

15 East 26th Street
New York
NY 10010

British Library Cataloguing-in-Publication Data
A catalogue record for this book is available from The British Library.

ISBN 08264 6590 0 (hardback)
      08264 6591 9 (paperback)

Typeset by BookEns Ltd, Royston, Herts.
Printed and bound in Great Britain by MPG Books Ltd, Bodmin, Cornwall

CONTENTS

For those who survived:
Mlentoo Wesley and Patricia Jabbeh Wesley, D.William and
Mary Tarty, Jasper and Tewah Ndaborlor

ACKNOWLEDGEMENTS

I was first sensitized to the issues of political identity when I was working in Liberia in 1987 and 1988 before the civil war there began. At the time I was a very inquisitive and naïve college student, asking many questions about what was happening politically and why everyone was so afraid. Many gracious Liberians spent time explaining the in and outs of ethnic political identification to me. Shortly after I left Liberia a vicious civil war began in which people were killed for who they were rather than for any political or ideological identification. Few of the people that I had known in Liberia were able to safely stay there. After the Liberian civil war I could not think in the same way again about ethnicity, nationalism and political identities. If this book is in any way educative about the nature of political identities, both those that are chosen and those that are imposed, it is because of the difficult lessons that I took to heart while witnessing the suffering of so many Liberian friends. It has become clear to me that if we are to understand why people around the world decide to kill one another in similar circumstances we need to understand well the critical issues of nationalism and political identity. This book is dedicated to those who survived the Liberian civil war.

It is my hope that this text will aid both undergraduates and generalists in ways of thinking about nationalism and political identities. I have to begin these acknowledgements by thanking the students I have taught in my courses on nationalism and ethnic conflict who have helped me with their questions and confusion as well as with their interest.

There are many others who deserve thanks for their help and encouragement to me as I embarked upon this project. While I was in the process of trying to decide whether I wanted to spend my time writing this book or working on other research projects, Michael Klare told me that it would simply be a 'good thing' to write the text. This was and has remained an encouragement to me as I spent the hours writing. Chip Hauss has been a resourceful and encouraging editor. I am especially thankful for his willingness to read through the whole text while it was still in the draft stage. I am grateful to Alison Hopkins and Andrea Ratzloff for their helpful research assistance and to the Wheaton College Alumni Grant program which provided me with research support at a critical time in the development of the manuscript. The attempt to effectively couch the case studies in their international context, a serious improvement to the text, resulted from the advice of my colleague Mark Amstutz and the example of Steve Lobell, Kristen Williams and their coauthors. Neal Carter lent his tremendous knowledge of Canada and uncompromising standards to me in commenting on the Quebec chapter. Jan Miller, Paul Joireman and Alexandra Webster have also aided me through their support and assistance as I have worked on this manuscript.

Identity and the Politics of Belonging

The Cold War ended and wars of ethnic nationalism began; or so it seemed to many observers of world politics at the turn of the twenty-first century. It appeared as if people stopped killing each other for ideological reasons, as they did during the Cold War, and started killing each other because of primal, deeply embedded hatreds. The power of ethnicity to mobilize people to action and threaten the state became visible to the world. The eruption of ethnic wars in Europe, Africa and Asia punctuated the fact that this was not a problem specific to the developing world, but a security threat to developed states as well.

Ethnicity is not new. It has deep historical roots and has manifested itself differently over time, reflecting the global, strategic environment. Ethnicity may have appeared dormant at different points in history only to revive again. Ethnicity is not new but the recognition of its role in international politics is. Over the past fifteen years we have witnessed an internationalization of ethnic conflict that has defied the boundaries of the state. This has been the case in Rwanda, the former Yugoslavia and even in Northern Ireland.

Many observers of the outbreak of ethnic violence around the world have attributed this violence to the existence of ancient hatreds, as if the mere presence of differences in identity between people groups were enough to drive them to violence. This, however, is not the case. There are too many examples of people groups living in close proximity for hundreds of years and never taking up arms against one another. An excellent example is that of the Flemish and Walloons in Belgium. How is it that these two peoples, as different as the Hutu and Tutsi in Rwanda, have never in the modern era had cause to go to war? The Flemish do not want to be Walloons and the Walloons do not want to be Flemish, but the two groups do not fight. The example of the Flemish and Walloons is typical of the peaceful coexistence of many different peoples and nationalities around the globe. Violent ethnic conflict is rare, and serious enough to merit close examination for its deviation from the norm of constructive dialogue and integration.

One of the goals of this text is to help the reader understand the critical difference between ethnicity as a *cause* of conflict and ethnic identity as a *mobilizing factor* in conflicts. While ethnic identities can lead people to see their personal interests as united with the interests

1

of a group, the mere existence of that group does not necessitate conflict.

WHO AM I?

A French-speaking Canadian
A New Yorker
A Scot
A Jew
A Latina

Consider how you might answer this question; possibilities abound. You could answer giving your race, sex, religion, heritage, generation, country of birth or political persuasion. Though it might not be immediately obvious, how you choose to answer this very simple question has strong political implications. Your answer will identify the group of people to whom you have the closest emotional and psychological attachment – the group to which you feel you belong. This may influence the way you vote in elections, the types of political activities in which you engage and even whether or not you would ever consider using violence or taking up arms against the state. We will discuss this in greater detail later on in the chapter, but for now, think about how you would answer these questions. Who are you? Why do you choose a particular identity? Why do you not choose other identities that might be available to you?

The types of identities that people choose for themselves tend to fall into a few categories: regional, religious, racial and linguistic. The study of ethnic identity is often referred to as *the politics of belonging*. We each decide for ourselves which identity is most important. We decide the group to which we belong. Because the decision is an individual one, not everyone finds each of these identities to be important. For example, though I speak English as my native language I do not see my interests as primarily tied to those of other English speakers. This is because there are so many English speakers and we are a majority in my country. I am more likely to see the dissimilarities between myself and other native English speakers, rather than the similarities.

Regional identities

A regional identity can be related to citizenship. For example, I may identify myself as Canadian because I live in Saskatchewan and hold a Canadian passport. However, identifying with the state is not necessarily the first identity choice for many. Some people, particularly those from culturally distinct areas, more readily identify themselves with a region rather than a country. For example, a Welshman might identify himself as Welsh before he would identify himself as British. Similarly, a woman may call herself French Canadian, or Quebecois, rather than referring to herself as just Canadian, because she feels a greater identification with those from Quebec. People from distinctive cities may identify themselves directly with that city before their region or their country. The most obvious example is New Yorkers; many of whom see New York as not only the centre of the world, but as culturally distinct from the rest of the United States. In the case of New York, the distinctiveness of the city is generally recognized, to the extent that other Americans, indeed people from other countries, understand that the moniker 'New Yorker' carries an identification of cultural distinctiveness. In fact, in all of these regional examples, the meaning is generally clear when a person refers to themselves as Welsh rather than British, and French Canadian rather than just Canadian. They are claiming the distinctiveness of that identity to define themselves. They are identifying the group to which they feel a sense of belonging.

Among immigrant groups around the world there is a second regional identity phenomenon, whereby people identify themselves with an ancestral homeland from which their parents or grandparents (or sometimes many further generations back) originally came. Someone may refer to himself or herself as Mexican, Irish or German without speaking the language of that country or perhaps having never seen it! This is somewhat unique to America as an immigrant country with a policy of granting citizenship to anyone born within its borders (*jus sanguinis*). Among immigrant groups in other countries of the world, this identification with an ancestral homeland is also evident.

Regional identities are most often those of the state of which people are a part. But they can also be that of a region within one's state, a city, or another state entirely; it is the psychological attachment of an individual rather than their specific location that matters most.

Religion

Religion is another identity that creates a sense of belonging for many people around the world. Religion, however, is slightly more controversial than a regionally defined identity. Consider the case of New Yorkers discussed previously. If I live in New York City but do not consider myself a New Yorker as my fundamental identity, that is not particularly problematic. However, it is problematic if I am a Jew, a Christian or a Muslim and I do not see this as critical to my identity. The difference arises because other adherents to my religion will know what I ought to believe or think or do. There will be those of my faith who may think that I am following the wrong path, that I am 'like a sheep that has gone astray'. Therefore, religion is slightly more complex because of the push for orthodoxy (correct beliefs), and/or orthopraxy (correct practices), among the adherents of any faith.

Race

Race is a peculiar case of ethnic identity. It is peculiar because there are many ways in which appearance signals ethnic identification: style of dress, hairstyle, particular types of jewelry or the presence or absence of facial hair in men. Race, however, is unusual, as it cannot be altered simply by changing clothes or hairstyles. It is an immediately perceptible outward appearance that is generally unchangeable throughout a person's lifetime.

In the nineteenth century, biologists divided the world into three racial groups. They identified people with light skin and fine hair as *Caucasian*. *Negroid* referred to people with darker skin and coarser hair and *Mongoloid* identified people with yellow skin and distinctive folds on the eyelids. These categories have since been abandoned as they are no longer useful. Indeed, they were of limited use even in the nineteenth century. They do not identify groups that are biologically similar, nor are they even very accurate in reflecting physical appearances. For example, some people who would have fallen into the category of Caucasian, such as Southern Indians, are far darker than people who would be called Negroids, such as light skinned Ethiopians or some African-Americans. Therefore, thinking in terms of racial categories is not biologically accurate nor particularly helpful in identifying ethnic groups.

Race only indicates ethnicity in particular contexts. For example, race would not allow a person to discern ethnicity for most European Union nationals, where the ability to identify whether someone is Irish, French or Belgian is more an issue of speech and dress than the colour of skin or hair. Even in the United States, where race would presumably identify darker-skinned individuals as African-Americans, rifts are developing. This is nowhere more obvious than in New York City, where West Indian and African immigrant populations increasingly see themselves as distinct from the wider black American population (Fears 2002). Throughout this book, race is treated as just another ethnic identity. It is discussed in that way because our understanding of race, like our understanding of ethnicity, is socially constructed. Let us discuss further what that means.

Scientists have never come up with any conclusive evidence to show that there is any such thing as race. Despite this fact, we all know what we are talking about when we discuss race. We know whether we are white or black or Asian or something else entirely. Even if a person is to consider herself of mixed race, she invariably knows how others view her and categorize her, based solely on her appearance. We know what race other people are; we can tell just by looking at them. Or can we? I used to think that it was possible to just look at someone and determine their race until I started meeting people who lived in South Africa under the apartheid regime. I remember quite clearly sitting through an academic presentation in the United States given by a South African man. He was discussing his work with the African National Congress (ANC) during the apartheid years. The ANC was known for its inclusiveness of anyone who opposed apartheid so it was not surprising to me that this man was white. However, during the question and answer period, a student asked the man how he had come to work with the ANC during the apartheid years as a white man. The speaker looked closely at the student and said, 'Am I white?' Well, he certainly passed my eyeball test, but in fact he was not classified as white by the apartheid regime, but as coloured. As a result, his educational opportunities were limited, he was only allowed to live in certain places and he had to carry a passbook. Not surprisingly, he joined the ANC in the struggles against a regime that would both label him and restrict his freedom based on such an arbitrary measure.

Conceptions of race are different across cultures. How could this be if race was an inborn trait, a fact or a concept that was agreed upon across cultures? If race was any of these things, people would just know what they were and there would be no confusion, but this is simply not the case. Once we try to move our conceptions of race across cultures and contexts, they fail. This is why sociologists tell us that race is socially constructed. It is something that is determined by a particular social or cultural context and not exclusively by the amount of melanin in your skin.

Language

In certain societies it is possible to find distinct linguistic groups that set the boundaries of belonging. Belgium is a society in which approximately 32 per cent of the population speaks French and another 58 per cent speaks Flemish or Dutch. The Belgians have found several creative ways of coping with this bifurcation of their society, including establishing a language line. North of the line, French is the language of commerce and education; south of it, Dutch is the language of commerce and education. Additionally, Belgium has developed a federal system in which power is shared between the two linguistic groups, with each having legislative and administrative responsibilities over the areas in which their language is dominant. These strategies have helped the Belgians to accommodate the diversity within their country while still maintaining a democratic and developed society. There are other countries which face similar linguistic divides in which language becomes the key identifying characteristic of distinct ethnic groups. One excellent example is

Canada, which has faced a secessionist movement from within the Francophone population of Quebec. The movement for the independence of Quebec has been violent on occasion and always virulent. Both the English-speaking and the French-speaking Canadians see a cultural and ethnic split that follows linguistic lines. It is language, rather than religion or region, which defines ethnicity in both Belgium and Canada.

Custom

Nearly all of the preceding categories could be captured under the category of custom, yet it is deserving of a separate category because of the fact that we see the use of particular customs establishing a divisive line in communities. This typically happens in cases where one ethnic group sees itself as the bearer or possessor of a more sophisticated or advanced culture, which really ought to be adapted by other groups for their own benefit. The Amhara in Ethiopia are one example. The Amhara have a long Christian history filled with beautiful works of art and architecture, ancient written manuscripts describing the correct actions of kings and religious leaders, and a long history of rule in Ethiopia. Many within the group see the Amhara as a bulwark against Islamic influences from the north and the south as well as the possessors of a rich culture that ought to be emulated by those individuals seeking a higher level of civilization. It is the culture and customs of the Amhara that separate them from other groups. They have formed their own distinctive identity on the basis of superiority. It is not necessary for a culture to see itself as superior in order to be separate or unique, though this usually contributes at some level. Separate cultures and customs are typically defined symbolically. It is worth a digression here to discuss the importance of symbols as signifiers of belonging as well as exclusion.

THE IMPORTANCE OF SYMBOLS

Symbols guard the borders of collective life. Symbols indicate who is 'us' and who is the other, or, as a sociologist might explain it, symbols identify who belongs to the in-group and who belongs to the out-group. In-groups are those groups with which an individual identifies psychologically. Out-groups are those groups of people with which an individual has no psychological affinity.

Symbols can be related to diet, etiquette, arts, rituals and language. For example, we can think of the different symbols that define the borders of religious groups in India. The importance of food taboos in both Hindu and Muslim cultures is one clear definition of the borders between these two groups. Hindus have a taboo against eating any beef products as the cow is religiously revered. Muslims are distinguished by their taboo against eating pork products. This distinction is further defined in the Muslim holy month of Ramadan, when not only are the traditional food taboos upheld, but Muslims fast throughout the entire month during the daylight hours.

Symbols are particularly important when in-groups and out-groups cannot be determined on the basis of physiognomy or physical appearance such as stature and skin colour. When two or more groups are similar in appearance, other identifiers must be used to establish in-group boundaries. A good example from the United States is the similarity of physiognomy between some Native Americans and people of Mexican descent. One might be able to generalize and say that on average Native Americans are taller, but beyond that the two groups are very similar in skin colour, hair colour and features. Yet, once we set aside these basic physical traits, there are many symbols that would set the two groups apart. Hairstyles in men are a particular indicator of difference between the two groups. In the Native American culture it is traditional for men to wear their hair very long. This is not at all the case with people of Mexican descent. Distinguishing the women of the two groups is more difficult, but might be possible through the identification of jewelry or beadwork that they might wear. These symbols of ethnic identity that would set Native Americans apart from Mexicans or other ethnic groups are all changeable. It is not necessary or in any way biological for Native Americans to wear their hair a certain way or to choose particular types of jewelry. When they choose to adopt these symbols of identification, they are identifying themselves as part of an in-group.

STRUCTURE OF THE BOOK

In the following pages of this book we will begin to investigate the issues of political identity and nationalism. In Chapter One the definitions of ethnicity and nationalism are presented. Three chapters which outline the basic themes follow: Chapter Two examines the oldest way of thinking about ethnicity – primordialism. In discussing primordialism we will be addressing the understanding of ethnicity that held sway through most of the twentieth century. This primordial understanding of ethnicity has been supplanted by two different approaches to ethnicity that we call instrumentalism and social constructivism. Instrumentalism and social constructivism are both relatively new approaches to understanding the politics of ethnicity that have arisen in the years following the Cold War. Instrumentalism is discussed in Chapter Three and social constructivism in Chapter Four. The third section of the book, which comprises Chapters Five through Eight, is a collection of case studies. Each case study gives a detailed description of a particular ethnic conflict and allows the reader to apply the theories discussed in the earlier chapters. The case studies have been selected both on the basis of geography and by the nature of the particular conflict. Therefore, the case of Quebec to illustrate ethnic conflict that is defined by the issue of language is included, and Yugoslavia to identify a case where ethnic conflict is defined by religion and culture, and so on. The case studies can be read on their own or in conjunction with the theoretical chapters. The theoretical chapters present multiple ways of interpreting the genesis of nationalist movements and the conduct of ethnic conflicts. The book concludes with a chapter on possible solutions to nationalist and ethnic conflicts.

Bibliography

Fears, D. (2002) 'A Diverse – and Divided – Black Community.' *The Washington Post*, February 24.

CHAPTER 1

Ethnicity and Nationalism

Nationalism joins culture and politics in a common purpose. It brings together the high-born and the low and gives those, even of the meanest circumstance, a pride in being able to feel one with the highest classes in the country, and in a common culture and history.

[Bell, 1975]

In this chapter the focus will be on defining what we mean by nationalism and ethnicity. While definitions are important in nearly every area of the social sciences, when we study political identity issues an unclear understanding of terms often leads to complete confusion. This is particularly true with regards to the word 'ethnicity', which in so many arenas has been incorrectly narrowed to refer only to people of racially defined minority groups.

WHAT IS ETHNICITY?

We have established that region, religion, language, custom and race can all be a part of a person's identity. These are the main contributors to a person's ethnic identity or *ethnicity*. Ethnicity is a somewhat new term, which did not come into common usage until the latter part of the twentieth century. Ethnicity is a term that is strongly contested in the academic literature. In the following section we will also be defining nationalism in some detail. The two terms are closely related and can be thought of as two sides of the same coin, with ethnicity being a benign manifestation of identity and nationalism a politicized shared identity.

 To clarify just what ethnicity entails, I will borrow and amend a list of the characteristics of ethnic groups from Hutchinson and Smith (1996).

Every ethnic group has:

- A proper name, such as 'Serbian', 'African-American' or 'Lebanese'.

- A myth of common ancestry. 'Myth' is a highly appropriate word because ethnicity is not concerned with the genetic realities of common ancestry, but rather with the popularized beliefs regarding ancestry.

9

- Shared historical memories. This can refer to events and celebrations, heroes or other common experiences.

- A common culture, defined by language or religion or customs or some mix of these three.

- A link with a geographic homeland.

- A sense of common cause or solidarity among some members of the population.

Ethnicity is subjective. It is constructed of memories, culture and a sense of solidarity – these hardly seem the things of which political movements are built. Yet, as noted earlier in the text, ethnicity is all about the politics of belonging. Emotional ties lead to a political identity that can be strong enough to lead people to take up arms against the state or another group.

The strength of ethnic identity or sentiment will be different among individuals of the same group. Moreover, everyone has a certain set of identities from which they can choose. Is it region, religion, heredity, race, or language that defines a person? The answer is that it depends. Thus, studying ethnicity is not simple because it is not as straightforward as studying citizenship or war between states, where it is absolutely clear to which state someone belongs. I may choose an ethnic identity that is not shared by my cousins or even members of my immediate family. My sister may consider herself to be Czech because she enjoyed all of the customs and celebrations of our childhood whereas I simply consider myself to be American because I found that very same shared culture to be annoying or lacking in meaning. Therefore, I can adopt common cultural practices of America and distance myself from the ethnic identity of the family of my birth.

Dual identities

The example presented above raises the question of the possibility of an individual having dual identities. Think about yourself and how you answered the identity question at the beginning of the book. Did you name a region and a religion? Many people capture two or three different ethnic identities. I can be an American and a Quaker or feel equally Welsh and British. It is wholly possible for a person to identify with several groups at the same time. This has been particularly true of groups in countries with strong regional identities, such as the Catalans in Spain, many of who consider themselves to be both Catalan and Spanish.

There are two circumstances that might lead an individual to select a particular ethnic identity as the primary group to which she belongs: 1) the presence of able leaders in support of the cause of a particular group, 2) the presence of economic or political incentives.

Leadership

Leaders are quite influential in their ability to promote the interests of a particular ethnic group. The reasons that leaders might have for championing the interests of an ethnic group are discussed in more detail in Chapter Two. Typically, a leader takes up the cause of an ethnic group in order to promote his or her own power, or to achieve a particular agenda.

Oppression

A second critical factor in identity choice has to do with economic or political oppression. Nationalism is intensified by the politics of exclusion. Any time a group of people feels particularly targeted for ill-treatment or oppression, there is a likelihood that their identification will turn from ethnic to national identity: in other words their identity will become politicized. If one group in a society is set apart for unequal treatment, either economically or politically, then the boundaries of that group become clearly defined. Thus, they define themselves as something else outside the dominant group. Those that remain in the oppressed group are typically those that have no choice because their identities are clearly defined for them via political or economic exclusion. For example, people of Chinese descent living in Indonesia suffer various forms of discrimination. They are not always allowed to buy land or houses, and even if they do so their property rights are not always respected. They are treated with suspicion and often find their freedom of movement restricted. They have frequently been the target of violence. These types of discrimination make it unlikely that, as generation passes to generation, Indonesians of Chinese descent will simply be integrated into the Indonesian common culture. In fact, the presence of discriminatory treatment over generations makes it more likely that people of Chinese descent will view themselves as distinct from other Indonesian citizens far into the future.

Ethnic conflict is related to economic development and economic development follows a pattern. Throughout history economic development has occurred in areas that have been favoured by the trading systems of their time. During the fourteenth and fifteenth centuries in Europe, economic growth was focused on the coastal areas along major trading routes. As these areas developed, cities formed and prospered. As the cities prospered so did the countryside surrounding the cities, as the demand for agricultural goods such as food and wool for clothing grew with the population of the cities. Europe is not the only example. The vast majority of China's population – 94 per cent – is concentrated in its coastal areas, where the large cities such as Beijing and Nanjing are located. The growth and prosperity of these cities leads to the growth and prosperity of China's inland areas.

Economic growth and prosperity tends to be concentrated regionally. Ethnic groups are also concentrated regionally. Most people who would identify themselves as Scottish live in the northernmost part of the United Kingdom. The Hausa live in the northern areas of Nigeria and are present in far fewer numbers in Southern cities and rural areas. Most Sikhs in India live in the state of Punjab.

Thus, there will be an inevitable coincidence of ethnicity and development or ethnicity and a lack of economic prosperity. It is the latter circumstance that is most concerning. A history of unequal development in a country in which the regional inequalities coincide with ethnicity can establish the precipitating factors for ethnic conflict. It can give a group of people a legitimate grievance that over time can escalate into ethnic conflict.

NATIONALISM

Nationalism is politicized ethnicity. In other words, it is an ethnic group with a political agenda. Following this idea, E.J. Hobsbawm has noted that 'Nationalism comes before nation' (Hobsbawm, 1990). An ethnic group must be somehow politically mobilized before it becomes a nation and that political mobilization occurs in the form of some sort of collective objective of recognition.

We can talk about groups being more or less national depending on what their aspirations might be. If they are simply seeking the recognition of a particular cultural distinctiveness then they are less national than a group wanting their own state. The Welsh in the United Kingdom have been very interested in establishing cultural distinctiveness and recognition. Not so a group such as the Tibetans, who seek far more than recognition. Many Tibetans are engaged in political activity aimed at establishing a state completely separate from China in which Tibetans would control the government. We call this the pursuit of self-determination. The case of Tibet makes a sharp contrast to Welsh attempts at cultural recognition within the existing British state structure. Both are nationalist but with very different goals. All nationalisms seek to promote the particular agenda of a nation.

Many nationalist movements do not aspire to the formation of their own state but are aimed at achieving some middle level aspiration such as local autonomy or, perhaps, control of a sub-unit of government within a federal system. The Welsh pursuit of recognition and political rights exemplifies this type of 'middle of the road' nationalism in which the aim is greater local autonomy short of independence. Because the state is not directly threatened by these types of nationalist demands, middle of the road nationalism can be accommodated relatively easily by a willing state and does not tend towards violence.

Our interest in nationalism stems from the fact that it so often leads to violence. Violent manifestations of nationalism in the 1990s and the early twenty-first century have been surprising in their brutality. The collapse of Yugoslavia and the attempt to establish states in which one ethnic group was in the majority led to the practice of 'ethnic cleansing'.

Ethnic Cleansing

The term 'ethnic cleansing' is new, though the practice is not. It involves singling out a particular ethnic group for brutality in the hope that its members will abandon their homes and leave the area, thus making it ethnically homogeneous and under the control of one group. This type of violence in which civilians, rather than members of the armed forces, are the targets results from the desire to both establish control of a territory and to ensure that the remaining population has a majority of people from a particular ethnic group and will, as a result, have political control.

Nationalist movements that seek self-determination will indisputably be at odds with their existing states. One stark fact about the system of states that has evolved in the world is that it encompasses most of the existing territory. There are few areas left to claim where a nation could establish a state – Antarctica or parts of Somalia. Since most nationalist groups want to control the territory in which they are presently located, their interests are necessarily pitted against those of the state. Few states are content to relinquish territory to nationalist groups without a fight. The American Civil War is a case in point; the secessionist movement of the South led to a war because the Union government did not wish to sacrifice territory to appease the Southern Confederacy. Nationalist movements, which have an independent state as their goal, will always have strong enemies. Clifford Geertz noted the threat of nationalism to the territorial integrity of the state: 'Economic or class or intellectual disaffection threatens revolution, but disaffection based on race, language, or culture threatens partition, irredentism, or merger, a redrawing of the very limits of the state, a new definition of its domain' (Geertz, 1963). Moreover, since a state has a monopoly on the use of force, those groups with aspirations to self-determination will find themselves opposing armies, tanks and the full organizational capacity of the state. It is no easy task to take on a state's army when you are a smaller group with less funding and military equipment. This inequality in capabilities is referred to as a power asymmetry, because one party to the conflict has so much more power than the other. What, then, can be done? How do nationalist groups bent on self-determination fight the superior power of the state?

The first, and least objectionable, way for a group to try and gain self-determination or some middle level of representation is through political tactics such as civil disobedience, lobbying and the public articulation of community goals. Most ethnic groups are able to pursue their goals through peaceful and political means. A political, nonviolent strategy was highly effective in the push for decolonization in India. Gandhi and Nehru led an extremely powerful and peaceful movement to get the British to 'Quit India'. Yet, the decolonization experience was a bit unusual in that the legitimacy of the state was questionable because it was foreign. Such techniques have proven less successful in independent states across the world. For example, there was a concerted effort to use civil disobedience and nonviolent techniques to protect the autonomy of Albanian Kosovars living in Yugoslavia before the Serb takeover of the province of Kosovo in 1999.

Kosovo

Prior to the outbreak of violent conflict in Kosovo a nonviolent civil disobedience campaign among the Kosovo Albanians was effectively contesting the forceful Serbian retention of Kosovo as a part of the disintegrated Yugoslavia. Ibrahim Rugova, an Albanian university professor in Kosovo, spearheaded this civil disobedience movement. A self-professed pacifist, he based his leadership of the movement on the examples of Mahatma Gandhi and Martin Luther King, Jr. In 1992, Rugova was elected president of the illegal Kosovo Albanian parliament, a legislative body established as a shadow to the Serbian state legislature. When violence began in March of 1999 it was initiated entirely by the Serbs, who felt threatened by the creation of the Kosovo Albanian parliament. The existence of the illegal parliament itself was such an effective form of civil disobedience that the Albanians believed that their interests were sufficiently represented; thus, they refrained from resorting to violence as a form of protest (Freedom House, 2000).

It is, however, not always the case that a group is able to achieve its objectives through peaceful means alone. Further events in Kosovo demonstrated the failure, in this instance, of a political or a nonviolent solution. When the Serbian armed forces went in and attempted to drive the Kosovar Albanians out of Kosovo, international intervention to protect the Kosovars followed. The justification for intervention was to support the human rights of the Kosovar Albanians and prevent a massive and destabilizing exodus of refugees from Kosovo into surrounding countries. Why did the Serbs attempt to drive out the Kosovar Albanians? The underlying reason as to why the Serbs intervened in Kosovo is similar to the reason they intervened in Bosnia – collective fear of the future, in this case a fear that they would completely lose both representation and control of territory. A collective fear of the future is the driving force behind many violent

ethnic conflicts (Lake and Rothchild, 1996) as groups that have been shut out of the political process in the past, or have themselves limited the participation of others, face uncertainty.

In addition to nonviolent protest actions, there are two violent strategies with which a group can use to fight for independence against the superior power of the state – guerilla warfare and terrorism.

Guerrilla Warfare

How do you both promote your cause of independence within the territory you wish to control and at the same time struggle against the military might of the state? The answer, first developed during the Chinese Communist Revolution, is guerrilla warfare. The Eritrean case detailed in Chapter Eight is one example of guerrilla warfare that we will be examining in-depth.

Guerrilla warfare is a two-pronged strategy. The first prong is military. The military strategy of guerrilla warfare is to harass the enemy until they become weary of fighting. The second prong to the strategy of guerrilla warfare is a political one – a battle for hearts and minds that goes on through public relations and working closely with the population in a particular region. Gaining the support of a region's population enables guerilla military operations and undermines government morale. Guerrilla warfare is designed to be a publicity campaign, social action and military strategy all rolled into one. It is therefore ideal for nationalist campaigns for self-determination where there may be a local population to convince of the wisdom of independence.

A contemporary example of a group using guerrilla warfare tactics to achieve regional autonomy is the Moro National Liberation Front (MNLF) in the Philippines.

The MNLF

The MNLF is dedicated to establishing an independent Islamic state in the southern part of the Philippine Island of Mindinao. The MNLF was formed in the late 1960s to demand better treatment for the Muslim minority Moro people. The MNLF launched a guerilla movement against the Philippine state because they lost control of their land and experienced diminished local autonomy under the Philippine state. They were ultimately successful in their goals; in 1990 the Philippine government established the Autonomous Region of Muslim Mindinao (ARMM), which the MNLF was able to administer. Unfortunately, the underlying complaints of the Moro – economic underdevelopment and a lack of institutional support from the government – persist. As a result, more radical Moro nationalist groups have formed including the Moro Islamic National Front (MINF), which is now engaged in peace talks with the government, and the Abu Sayyaf organization. Abu Sayyaf desires the formation of an Islamic state with Shari'a law in southern Minidao and is using guerrilla warfare and terrorism to pursue its political goals. For example, in 2000, Abu Sayyaf captured 40 foreigners, held them for ransom, and upon receiving the ransom money, used it to buy 'a large cache of advanced weaponry and gear' (Yom, 2001).

Using a strategy of guerilla warfare requires a large number of supporters and a highly structured organization. These types of resources are not always available to a nascent group. As a result, guerilla warfare is often used in conjunction with, or following the use of, terrorism.

Terrorism

The terrorist attacks against the United States since 2000 exemplify the relative effectiveness of terrorism in challenging the power of a state that is far better financed and equipped than a particular dissident group. We find it objectionable and morally offensive that terrorism is used against innocent civilians in order to promote a political cause. However, historically, it has proved to work well in gaining publicity for the grievances of a particular group of people as well as fomenting revolutionary fervour to push for self-determination. The Greek historian Xenophon, writing in the third century BC, noted how psychological warfare and intimidation worked well against the enemy (1932). This is the same idea that is used today in terrorism.

Terrorism, because it is unexpected and targets the civilian population rather than the armed forces, is designed to instill fear in a population. In nationalist conflicts that fear is intended to lead to the release of a particular population from the control of the state or to otherwise achieve their agenda.

There are several current examples of the use of terrorism in the pursuit of nationalist causes. The Irish Republican Army in Northern Ireland, Hamas in Palestinian, ETA in Spain, the LTTE in Sri Lanka and Al-Itihad Al-Islamiya, a Somali group in Ethiopia have all used terrorist tactics to promote the goals of a particular group with long-standing political and economic grievances against the state.

Responding to terrorist violence is exceedingly difficult as it is necessary to first find the perpetrators in order to punish them. A state cannot, therefore, respond in the same way as it would if violent acts were perpetrated by a sovereign state. We know how to find states.

CONCLUSION

Ethnicity is a critical part of political identity. It can be formed on the basis of a variety of characteristics from region to religion. Ethnicity is so critical to political identity because we act politically based on the group with which we identify. At times groups cease to be content within the political system and begin to agitate for greater group rights or even independence. When this happens we say that the group has become nationalist. They have adopted a common political identity and their ethnicity is no longer just a cultural or social identifier. Now that the troublesome issue of definitions is addressed, it is possible to move on to a discussion of theories and cases.

Bibliography

Bell, D. (1975) 'Ethnicity and Social Change', in *Ethnicity: theory and experience*, edited by D. P. Moynihan. Cambridge, MA: Harvard University Press.

Freedom House. (2001) *Yugoslavia: Kosovo* (Website). Freedom House, June 15, 2001, 2000 (cited November 15, 2001). Available from http://216.119.117.183/research/freeworld/2001/countryratings/zzkosovo.htm

Geertz, C. (1963) 'Primordial Sentiments and Civil Politics in the New States', in *Old Societies and New States*, edited by C. Geertz. New York: The Free Press of Glencoe.

Hobsbawm, E.J. (1990) *Nations and Nationalism Since 1780, Canto*. New York: Cambridge University Press.

Hutchinson, J. and Smith. A.D. (1996) *Ethnicity*. New York: Oxford University Press.

Lake, D.A. and Rothchild, D. (1996) Containing Fear. *International Security* 21 (2):41–75.

Xenophon. (1932) *Anabasis: Books IV–VII, Symposium and Apology*. London: William Heinemann.

Yom, S. (2001) *The Two Worlds of Abu Sayyaf* [www.fpif.org]. Foreign Policy in Focus, 2001 (cited August 2001).

CHAPTER 2

Primordialism

One is bound to one's kinsman, one's neighbor, one's fellow believer, ipso facto; as the result not merely of personal affection, practical necessity, common interest, or incurred obligation, but at least in great part by virtue of some unaccountable absolute import attributed to the very tie itself.
[Clifford Geertz 1963]

Primordialism – the very word evokes images of ancient beginnings, evolution and a natural state of being. These are the images that most closely represent the primordialist view of ethnic identities. If the study of nationalism and ethnic conflict can be divided into new and old ideological approaches then primordialism would be in the 'old' camp both rhetorically and theoretically. It is 'old' rhetorically because most primordialists view ethnicity as defined by or intimately connected with blood ties or kinship.

The Rwandan Genocide

In 1994 the majority Hutu population in Rwanda organized themselves and in the course of two months proceeded to murder 800,000 Tutsi people living among them – the overwhelming majority of the Tutsi population. The genocide was conducted in a methodical way, often through the leadership of the local town governments. Hutus were encouraged to kill their ethnic Tutsi neighbours as a collective action for the public good. The underlying causes of this violence were differences between the two ethnic groups that were both ancient and sustained. The Hutus and Tutsis in Rwanda were unable to live together in peace because their inherent ethnic identities set them at odds with each other.

This type of explanation of the Rwandan genocide – one of the most notable, efficient and evil examples of ethnic based violence observed in recent times – is primordial. Primordialism assumes that a person's fundamental ethnic identity is fixed at birth and cannot change.

Primordialists view ethnicity as historically rooted because it is defined by descent or by family ties. It is also tied to geography or to a particular homeland. The geographic nature of the primordialist perspective arises because kinship groups, or those groups with blood ties, are generally restricted by natural boundaries that separate people such as mountains, rivers and forests. Natural boundaries define the traditional homelands of specific ethnic groups and traditional homelands are evocative symbols to ethnic groups, though they might have left them generations ago.

The end of the Cold War led to the emergence of multiple conflicts within states fought on the basis of ethnicity or with the purpose of ethnic cleansing. By combining the evidence from these conflicts with what was already known regarding ethnicity there emerged a consensus among scholars rejecting primordialism in favour of an understanding of ethnicity that accounts for more flexible identities. Ethnic wars, particularly in Bosnia and Rwanda, opened the eyes of the world to the type of destruction and violence that could be wrought in the name of ethnicity. The average person on the street would immediately understand and perhaps be sympathetic to the primordialist argument. Yet, the primordialist view is not dominant among scholars. Increasingly it is the case that scholars of ethnicity view ethnic identities as changeable. In spite of the fact that few scholars today find it credible, primordialism attempts to address the roots of ethnic identity and the reasons for its tremendously strong pull in the lives of modern as well as ancient peoples. Whether one accepts the primordialist point of view or not, it is influential in identifying the enduring strength of ethnic ties and the commitment with which they are held. Therefore, it is worth considering this position in-depth.

Primordialists do not view ethnic identification and nationalism as modern phenomena. Nations are seen as old; rooted in both human biology and historical antiquity. This belief in the age and strength of ethnic groups gives primordialists a unique and sometimes very helpful perspective on ethnic conflict. For example, primordialists are less likely to think of the end of the Cold War as giving rise to greater ethnic conflict because of the formation of new ethnic groups and new nationalist causes. Instead, they would view the origins of ethnic groups as dating much further back historically. Primordialists view the Cold War as a time in which ethnic sentiment gave way to ideological issues, allowing the nationalist conflicts to reappear when the ideological conflict of the Cold War ended. For primordialists then, ethnic groups and the rise of nationalist agendas is neither surprising, nor in need of much explanation, as it is something that has always been a source of conflict.

Primordialists believe that ethnic identities are determined at birth by the ethnic identities of the parents, and are unchangeable. Ethnicity is an ascribed trait, like a person's sex or age. Some primordialists are more rigid about this belief than are others; a few are even willing to grant that under very particular circumstances it might be possible for a person to change ethnic identities. For example, at a young age, when a person is more able to adapt culturally and linguistically, a child may adopt a new ethnic identity. However, even the most flexible primordialists would argue that the realistic opportunities for a person to change ethnic identity are slim. The belief that ethnic identities are fixed and unchangeable sets primordialists apart from other theorists of ethnicity and nationalism.

Though there is an acceptance within primordialism of the ever-present nature of ethnic groups, there is a great deal of disagreement as to whether it is biology, history or some form of culture that defines the boundaries between various ethnic groups. This chapter will be divided up into several sections based upon the different primordialist perspectives. At one extreme is the biological perspective, which argues that ethnic sentiment, or ethnocentrism, is a natural, inborn characteristic of human beings. Ethnic group identification is a result of the process of the Darwinian 'survival of the fittest'. In the middle are those primordialists who argue that culture or language fix our ethnic identities and that they cannot be changed. At the other end of the primordialist spectrum lies the group that we refer to here as the 'soft primordialists', that school which rejects the strict definitions of the biology, culture and language groups in favour of a primordialism that emphasizes the importance of myth and history.

BIOLOGICAL OR NATURAL PRIMORDIALISM

The belief that ethnic identification arises from something inherent in the biology of human beings is the first form of primordialism we will examine in this chapter. It is appropriate to begin here because when this group of scholars discusses primordialism they are truly going back to the 'primordial soup' and examining the development of ethnic identification as a kind of evolutionary natural selection. Those who argue this point of view are called sociobiologists. Sociobiologists believe that ethnic identification and ethnic conflict are everywhere a fact of life, among animals as well as people, and that the propensity to favour close kin groups is genetic in both humans and animals. Ethnic conflicts exist across the spectrum of modernized, developed countries from ethnic cleansing in the former Yugoslavia, to race riots in the United Kingdom and complaints of reverse discrimination in the United States. These examples of ethnic conflict across all levels of industrialization and development and in virtually every society have caused sociobiologists to look past cultural or political explanations to a biological explanation of ethnic identity.

Sociobiologists attempt to use scientific approaches, such as Darwinian natural selection, evolutionary biology, and genetics, to explain social behavior in a way that the social sciences do not. For example, sociobiologists might try to explain the movement of societies from a band type of political organization to a kingdom or an organized state by a combination of biological research and theoretical principles derived from the natural sciences. They work from the assumption that the species that survive the evolutionary process in all living creatures are those that are best at producing healthy offspring. However, it is important that we think about this not just in terms of the survival of a particular family but also in terms of what is 'socially helpful to the reproductive success of relatives such as brothers, sisters, cousins, nephews and nieces, all of whom carried proportions of their own genes' (Reynolds, Falger and Vine, 1987). Thus, we are not only considering evolutionary effects on individuals but also on larger kin groups. It is by theorizing regarding larger kin groups that sociobiologists can arrive at the influence of biology in the development of ethnocentrism.

Ethnocentrism:

Belief in the superiority of one's ethnic group. Ethnocentrism usually involves a positive approach to the in-group and a negative attitude towards members of an out-group.

Both animals and people tend to define their social environment in terms of their in-group and their out-group. An in-group is the close community or the 'family' who is us. You take care of those in your in-group and ignore the needs of those in your out-group. In animals these groups are defined on the basis of genetics alone. In human beings the definition is clearly more complex and is affected by cultural, economic and political circumstances. Sociobiologists offer an understanding of ethnic identity, and more specifically of ethnocentrism, that is based on an impulse present in human beings biologically as well as culturally.

As early as 1871, anthropologists noted the importance of ethnocentrism in identifying different social rules that apply to in-groups and out-groups (Tylor, 1871). As an example, in 1943, a thirty-year old, white, American man woke up one morning feeling very angry and depressed. After getting dressed and eating his breakfast he picked up a gun and left the place where he was living. By mid-afternoon he had killed two men. When the deaths of these two men were reported to the authorities, no action was taken. The next day the man did the same thing, this time killing only one person. Again, no action was taken against him. No action was taken against him because the government supported his actions. The man in this example was a soldier on a battlefield in World War II who was just doing his duty. He would never be punished for his actions and might actually be rewarded. As a society we would not view this killing as murder because it occurs against members of an out-group or, what we call in politics, an enemy. In 1943 there were specific social rules for dealing with members of an out-group on the battlefield. Tylor believed that the cultural definition of murder which allows for lawful killing in warfare is an indication of ethnocentrism. In warfare we kill our enemies, but we do not call it murder because they are not us.

The sociobiological argument regarding ethnicity is that kin selection promotes the fitness or survivability of the kin group. In laymen's language this means that people have a propensity to favour the interests of their relatives. When people favour their kin in social relationships, they and their family are stronger. The strength of these family groups, or, to use a biological term, their 'fitness', relative to groups that do not have strong kinship ties, makes strong kin groups more likely to survive the process of natural selection. Since kin groups have evolved into what we now consider to be ethnic groups, there is a biological explanation for the presence of ethnocentrism.

Sociobiologists are coming from the most rigid of the primordialist approaches because of their belief in a biological explanation for ethnic sentiments. Other primordialists also believe in the power of ethnocentrism, but see these attitudes as learned in childhood rather than driven by biology (Reynolds, Falger and Vine, 1987). Still others are willing to accept the relevance of the sociobiological contributions to the study of ethnicity, but do not see them as a sufficient explanation of ethnic identities that turn nationalistic. James Kellas views identity as part genetics and part contextual, arguing that 'Human nature provides the necessary condition for ethnocentric behavior, but politics converts this into the sufficient conditions for nationalism as we understand it today' (Kellas, 1998).

Human beings are violent by nature

Sociobiologists have argued that it is in the nature of human beings to go to war, to turn to violence as a solution to problems, to fight. Certainly there are many examples of such behaviour in our history as human beings to support this approach. Particularly interesting is the evolutionary point of view here. If it is in the nature of human beings to fight and use violence against one another then we have certainly perfected the techniques for doing so as human history has moved forward through time. Our weapons have moved from the primitive to the sophisticated. At each step along the way there has been an emphasis on creating the most efficient weapons – efficient in terms of killing the most people in the least amount of time. From the primordial approach, violence is inevitable, what changes are the justifications for its use.

Nationalism is a very useful tool for the individuals or the state to justify violence against others. Nationalism simply helps to explain why some people believe that violence is necessary. This is a type of rationalization, to be sure, but one that is common to man.

> Men and women first construct towering structures of theology and religion, complex analyses of racial character and class structure, or moralities of group life and virility before they kill one another. Thus they fight for Protestantism or Mohammedanism, for the emancipation of the world proletariat or for the salvation of the Nordic culture, for nation or for king. Men will die like flies for theories and exterminate each other with every instrument of destruction for abstractions. (Durbin and Bowlby, 1938)

The language quoted here may be old, but the sentiment is just as relevant as ever. Human beings have a need to justify our frequent turns to collective violence. Religion will do, as will theories of political power and/or ties to a particular ethnic group. If one views human nature as inevitably violent, then seeing nationalist sentiments used to justify that violence is not particularly surprising.

CULTURAL PRIMORDIALISM

A second approach to primordialism is one that emphasizes culture as the critical tie that binds people together. This is distinctly different from the strictly biological position. Most of the authors who are situated in this camp end up being called primordialists because they view culture as interwoven with ethnicity and ethnicity as inborn. This is a type of primordialism in which the emphasis is not on the biological trait, but instead on the results of being of a particular group with all of its attendant social practices, language, religion, etc.

The most famous of all the primordialists supporting this point of view is Clifford Geertz, an anthropologist who wrote on the importance of culture in forming ethnic identities. Geertz built on the work of Edward Shils (1996) who discussed the primordial ties of small groups of individuals as fundamental to human community. Geertz argues that every individual is born into a particular culture that structures his beliefs and his identity. From the perspective of Geertz, people view their own cultural background as primordial, and thus it is. Culture is important insofar as people claim it to be a foundational identity. There is a connection between extended family members that is based on more than simply the ties of blood. A common religion, language and customs serve to bring people together into ethnic groups. These similarities give people a common interest and, at some point, common political goals as well. Geertz's research with many people groups led him to believe that people give their ties of origin, ancestral territory or homeland, descent and kin group a value which supercedes all others in forming their identity. Since these facts of origin and ancestral homeland cannot be changed they are fixed and influential throughout the lives of people all over the world. Yet, for Geertz, these are only the causes of the ties that bind people together.

> One is bound to one's kinsman, one's neighbor, one's fellow believer, *ipso facto*; as the result not merely of personal affection, practical necessity, common interest, or incurred obligation, but at least in great part by virtue of some unaccountable absolute import attributed to the very tie itself. (Geertz, 1963)

These ties do not change over time. However, Geertz argues that the strength of ethnic ties varies from place to place. In fact, we can identify a division in the world between old and new states in the way in which ethnic identity is manifest. In old states, those that have been independent for quite some time, such as France, Britain and even the United States, ethnicity is managed by the state and people are less likely to view their ethnic ties as more important than their state loyalties. In these old states, a civic nationalism has replaced ethnic nationalism.

In other words ethnicity has been superceded by an identification with the state. Geertz argues that this is an effect of modernity. New states – we can think of most of the states in the developing world as belonging to this category – still have to contend with the problems of ethnic nationalism because they have not yet become fully modern.

Ethnic and Civic Nationalisms

Ethnic nationalism is an identity based on objective criteria, such as language or descent. Those included in a group fall into it almost by default. At the same time, those that find themselves outside the group do not have the means to join the group. Individuals are unable to choose their ethnic group but are instead assigned their ethnic groups from birth. Ethnic nationalism calls on mobilization of those people whose characteristics are chosen for them. Ethnic nationalism does not necessarily follow the lines of the state; therefore, multiple ethnic nations within a state can lead to the fracturing of the state, as seen in the former Yugoslavia.

> Civic nationalism, on the other hand, is grounded in subjective choices that an individual makes. Nations are defined in territorial and legal terms, and citizens need only adhere to the political structures that govern a nation to be considered a part of it. Civic nationalism is seen in multi-nation states such as the United States, where a variety of ethnic groups rally together under the ideology of the civic nation. Patriotism is civic nationalism.

Geertz argues that 'new states are abnormally susceptible to serious disaffection based on primordial attachment' (Geertz, 1963). Ethnic sentiments set themselves up in direct conflict with the civic nationalism of the state. Competing loyalties to the state threaten the state with the loss of territory if a sub-state group were to secede or threaten secession.

This presents a particular problem in new states, which have to contend with this 'serious disaffection' while at the same time addressing the concern of their populace for economic and political development and trying to promote the goals and policies of the state. These are not easy tasks to accomplish, and the successful achievement of these goals is dependent on the presence of a strong state. New states, however, are unlikely to be strong and more likely to face demands from ethnic groups. If we consider the fact that most African countries did not become independent until the 1960s, perhaps it is not so surprising that there appears to be a conflict between the state and various ethnic groups seeking to promote their own interests. In these states, and all young states, Geertz notes the conflicting demands to maintain a politically powerful personal identity and the need to construct a powerful national community. However, Geertz's theorizing in this regard does not help us to understand increasing nationalism in the former Yugoslavia or among the Quebecois (Canada) or the Basques (Spain), or the Welsh, or the Scottish (United Kingdom).

Geertz is particularly helpful in understanding the role that culture can play in organizing identity. Whether you support the primordial position of Geertz or not, his writing is useful in pointing to the ways identity is formed. Churches, religious associations and religious schools are powerful transmitters of cultural identity in every society. To the extent that people identify with these institutions, they will share similar identities with others who do so. Additionally, when churches and religious associations are strong and deeply embedded within the culture, they will be most effective at transmitting that culture from generation to generation. Geertz argues that ethnic ties are more particular to new nations because of the focus of modern states on turning these strong ties of custom, language and religion into allegiance to a civil state over time. For Geertz, it is not so much the primordial ties of birth and origin that are important, but the meaning that individuals attach to those ties and to the importance of belonging to a group.

LINGUISTIC PRIMORDIALISM

While some primordialists see language as somehow captured under the general understanding of culture, others view it as critical to the definition of identity. Language is universal. It is a more obvious identifier of ethnic origin than religion or culture. With a few exceptions, such as English and Spanish, it is also geographically concentrated in a way that religion and race are not.

In many previously colonized countries around the world there are a variety of languages spoken in the home. These languages are what we call 'mother tongues' because we learn them on our mother's knee. However, in countries such as India, Nigeria and Malaysia, the language of the colonizing country, typically English or French, becomes the language of business and governmental activity. Jean Laponce finds that languages can contribute to conflict, particularly when they are used in the same contexts (Laponce, 1985). He argues that when different languages are used by ethnic groups, but those languages do not serve the same role, they do not contribute to conflict. When one language is used at home and another for business there is no inherent conflict. However, when there is a linguistic competition – when languages are used in the same context – they define ethnicity and can become a source of conflict. Laponce writes in reference to the Canadian context, where, in Quebec, there have been competing languages in the commercial realm: English and French.

One excellent example of the power of language and the salience of linguistic issues in politics is India. In India there are two national languages: English and Hindi. There are also a wide variety of languages used at the state level. The different Indian states use different languages, such as Gujarati and Bengali, because a majority of their populations speak these languages. Understanding the language of government is a concern for citizens of any state, as the state affects our lives in so many ways: payment of taxes; registration of births, deaths and marriages; and litigation for example. Recognizing the power of language and the necessity of understanding the working of the local governments, the Indian Constitution also makes provision for the formation of new states should a need arise. This constitutional provision has the effect of allowing for further linguistic diversity. Language is politically important in constructing identities and setting political agendas.

Brain biology and language

Some scholars have noted a biological differentiation based on mother tongue or multiple language use (Albert and Obler, 1978; Tsunoda, 1978). Tadanobu Tsunoda has noted the biological differences in the brains of Japanese and the brains of Westerners. Tsunoda has posited that the brains of the Japanese are shaped by the learning and use of the Japanese language as a mother tongue. The biological distinctiveness that ensues from the learning of particular languages, or of multiple languages, has two cultural applications. First of all, language affects personality, and secondly, language influences the cohort of people with whom one feels a sense of familiarity both because of the language itself and because of the fact that we tend to seek out those that we understand. This is particularly true for the people who provide goods and services to us. It is important to be able to understand your mechanic, your doctor and even your plumber, because the clarity of communication with these people can affect the outcomes of their services and the quality of your life.

Language can define the borders of ethnicity, and it can influence both the culture and personality of a group of people. Because of its importance in defining identity there are those in the primordialist school of thought who are there because of the distinct role they see language playing in the formation of ethnicity.

'SOFT' PRIMORDIALISM

So far, the types of primordialism we have considered stress either blood ties or culture in the formation of bonds of identity that are resistant to change. There is yet another type of primordialism, which I refer to as 'soft' primordialism because it views the primordial attachments as evolving from history and a myth of a common homeland rather than blood ties or cultural heritage. Essentially, this means that the defining elements of ethnic identification are psychological and emotional rather than biological. However, both the biological primordialists and the 'soft' primordialists view ethnicity as innate and unchangeable. Anthony Smith notes the 'extraordinary persistence and resilience of ethnic ties and sentiments, once formed' (Smith, 1986). This is a separate category from cultural and linguistic forms of primordialism because these elements are not viewed with the same importance. Instead, the most convincing thing to most primordialists in this category is the importance of shared beliefs and myths of origins.

One of the 'soft' primordialists, Walker Connor, refers to a nation as 'a group of people who believe they are ancestrally related' (Connor, 1994). Whether the group of people is actually related by blood or not is unimportant – as long as they believe it to be true. They must have a myth of common descent, which then gives rise to a number of secondary issues such as the importance of the ancestral homeland and cultural issues. Anthony Smith refers to each national unit or ethnic community as an *ethnie*. Smith believes that each *ethnie*, or ethnic community, is rooted in history, insofar as the shared meanings and experiences of individuals are passed down and crystallized through generations of people. This 'passing down through the generations' occurs through religious practices, certain

types of dress, language and art (Smith, 1986). Both Connor and Smith emphasize the degree to which this national sentiment takes the form of cultural myths and symbols.

Interestingly, Walker Connor argues that it is very difficult for Americans to understand the concept of belonging to a nation since they, by and large, do not share either emotional and psychological ties to an ancestral homeland or a myth of common descent. He argues that America is unusual in this regard and that the fact that most Americans conceive of themselves as Americans even though their roots are elsewhere has two effects. First of all, the lack of understanding of ancestral ties means that Americans have difficulty comprehending the nationalist sentiments of groups of people like the Scottish, Vietnamese or Hausa, which have a strong sense of ethnic identity and an understanding of their own roots in their ancestral homeland. The second problem of the American experience is that rather than viewing the American assimilation model as anomalous, most Americans, and even scholars of nationalism from other countries, can fall into the trap of assuming that the American model is the norm, when instead it is the exception.

Anthony Smith ventures into the theoretical territory of explaining the dissolution or disappearance of ethnic groups as well as their persistence. Looking back into history Smith notes that some ethnic groups, such as the Assyrians, were present in the ancient world but have since disappeared. Smith posits that this is a result of assimilation of the cultural and religious practices of other ethnic groups combined

with a state that was seeking to grow at the expense of other institutions within the polity (Smith, 1986). Thus, we can imagine that those groups that lend themselves well to the assimilation of another culture or a dominant culture and have no political entity protecting their specific interests may, in fact, loose their ethnic group definition over time. Here the example of the Native Americans in the United States is also salient. Theirs is an ethnic group in which many assimilated into the dominant culture; the pressures and enticements of that culture and the genocide of their people lead to the destruction of the political and social structures that had existed before European settlers arrived in the United States.

NEOPRIMORDIALISM?

Samuel Huntington has argued that, with the end of the Cold War we will no longer see the kind of ideological conflict that characterized both World War II and the whole post-Cold War era, in which the world was divided into two spheres on the basis of ideology. During the Cold War, the United States led the democratic camp and the Soviet Union the communist one. With the collapse of the Soviet Union, ideology does seem to have lost its importance as a force for political motivation. Huntington has argued that in the new century conflict will no longer be between states, but we will begin to see what he calls a 'Clash of Civilizations' – a situation in which the world is divided up into camps on the basis of what he refers to as the great civilizations of Asia, the West and the Islamic World. Huntington argues that civilizations are defined on the basis of religion, physical characteristics and culture. He identifies the major contemporary civilizations as follows: Sinic, Japanese, Hindu, Islamic, Western, Latin American and possibly African (Huntington, 1998: 45–7). Huntington posits that with the waning of the importance of ideology people will return to more basic and traditional identities in the way they order their worlds. He argues that we can think of these civilizations in the context of the world system and evaluate how they balance each other. The United States should thus begin to think of its own interests as coterminous with those of other Western countries and opposing those of other civilizations.

This type of thinking is a kind of neoprimordialism. It is distinctly different from other primordialist accounts, which would not see ethnicity as ever having been irrelevant. However, it operates from the same type of premise as traditional primordialist approaches because Huntington views people as having such strong emotional ties to ethnicity that they will begin to organize themselves around these ethnic issues in opposition to other groups. What is somewhat confusing in Huntington is the reason why he picks such broad categories. Similarities in the Islamic world begin to break down quickly when we look more closely into the different political structures that exist, linguistic differences and the split between Sunni and Shi'ite sects within Islam. These are issues that have caused divisions in the Islamic world in the past and will probably continue to do so.

The relevance of Huntington's argument regarding the clash of civilizations will have to be judged in the long term. A myriad of clearly defined ethnic groups and identities already exist within the 'civilizations' Huntington notes. Given the fact that most primordialists view these separate and smaller groups as immutable, his position will be controversial even within the primordialist camp.

CRITICISMS OF THE PRIMORDIALIST APPROACH

Traditional primordialist approaches such as those of Smith, Geertz and Connor have been subject to four specific criticisms that have led many to dismiss primordialism as naïve or unable to explain the complexity of ethnic identifications. The first problem is that most primordialists have not wanted to associate themselves too closely with the idea that blood ties are important. There are reasons for wanting to shy away from this issue. Few would like to be associated with the racist ideas of ethnicity that motivated the Holocaust in the Second World War and the German emphasis on the supremacy of the Aryan race – a belief based on the importance of blood ties. Thus, many primordialists have been unwilling to go as far as the sociobiologists, who command only a weak following, and argue the importance of nature and biology. Those who wish to support a different sort of primordialism without any emphasis on the importance of blood ties or natural selection have found themselves in the much more precarious position of asserting the primordialism of cultural identification or language. This is a weaker position because it is clearly easier to learn traditions and languages than it is to develop a genetic tie, thereby weakening the argument that forms the basis of primordialism.

The second problem with the primordial position is that if ethnicity is truly primordial then it cannot change. Primordialism assumes that there are certain underived aspects of identity, such as culture and language, which form the ethnic identities of people. Yet, we know that ethnic identifications can come and go between, and even within, generations – that ethnicity is fluid. It is possible, and indeed it has occurred with some frequency, for a person to be raised in America with American parents and attend college in America and then move to Israel and become an Israeli citizen, over time completely adapting to that new situation, politically, linguistically and culturally. In essence, it is possible for someone to be born and raised in one culture and then choose another. Moreover, some ethnic identifications can be very strong under certain circumstances and completely disappear in other contexts. I used to teach at a college in Western New York State and many of my students were of Irish descent. Some of them identified very strongly with Irish causes and Irish traditions. They identified themselves as Irish – until they left the United States. Once in a setting in which they clearly stood out as Americans, they began to see themselves and their ethnic background in different ways. Many of us have had this experience. In our own countries we rail at the government and criticize the culture. Yet when we find ourselves in another culture, in another country, we pine for home and what was an irritation only seems sweet with the longing for familiarity. If ethnicity is primordial, then how can it be contextual? If ethnicity is primordial then how can it change? Moreover, if ethnicity is primordial it should not be possible for new ethnic groups to be 'created'. Yet this is precisely what happened in many areas of the world that experienced colonization as the colonial governments attempted to divide and rule the people of the territories they claimed. It is this type of criticism that causes people to dismiss the sociobiologists because presumably any genetically ingrained behaviour would not be subject to change.

A third criticism of primordialism is that it cannot explain the issue of multiple ethnic identities. This is particularly problematic in the American context in which people may have a wide variety of ethnic identities and choose among them or exercise particular ethnic identities in particular contexts. One example of this issue in America is the renowned golfer, Tiger Woods.

Tiger Woods

His mother is from Thailand and his father is an African-American. So what is he? His physiognomy suggests African-American, but culturally he is mixed. He grew up eating his mother's Asian cooking and half of his extended family is Asian. Certainly this had the effect of passing on some of the cultural traditions of his mother. Woods describes himself as 'proudly multiracial' and does not like to be categorized as either African-American or Asian-American because he is both. It is a challenge to primordialists to come up with explanations describing people like Woods who clearly carry multiple ethnic identities.

A fourth criticism of primordialism is that it is difficult to distinguish whether primordial ethnic ties are in fact primordial, and in that way, different from other types of social ties and social experiences. Primordialism has often been reduced simply to emotion, though if one was to believe the sociobiologists this would be genetically generated emotion. However, if this is the case then there is nothing primordial about ethnic identities, as our emotions derive from the bonding process we experience as infants and through our movement as individuals through identity formation during our adolescent years. Emotions do not emerge solely from our genetic makeup. Thus, any claim of emotionalism undermines the assertion that ethnic identities are primordial.

These criticisms have led many to abandon the theory of primordialism and have led to the ascendancy of both the social constructivist and the instrumentalist points of view. Those who still favour the primordialist approach, particularly within the sociobiology camp, argue that, though it is true that ethnic identities can change over time, they cannot appear from nowhere. Ethnic conservatism is so strong that only in rare circumstances will someone have enough individual incentive to change. Even then the choice pool is distinctly limited. From the primordialist perspective, it is simply not possible for someone who is born in rural Brazil to a Catholic family to choose to be a Quebecois. Pierre van den Berghe, a well-known primordialist, has argued that 'Ethnicity can be *manipulated* but not *manufactured*. Unless ethnicity is rooted in generations of shared historical experience, it cannot be created *ex nihilo*' (van den Berghe, 1981).

Theoretically, primordialism has been eclipsed by a new consensus in the social sciences supporting social constructivism or instrumentalism as the ideological approach of choice. This consensus has evolved as social scientists have grappled with the changing ethnic landscape of the new century. In several cases where there were previously single states, multiple states now exist: Slovenia, Croatia, Bosnia and Serbia and Montenegro where the former Yugoslavia used to be; Somaliland, Puntland and Somalis where the former Somalia used to be.

However, it should be clear from this chapter that ethnicity is not some sort of historical anachronism. It is not a problem of developing countries, nor is it a simple explanation for differing cultural traits and customs. Ethnicity is so compelling that sociobiologists look for a biological explanation as to why people hold their ethnic identities so dear. Ethnicity allows people to define the borders of the group of which they are a part. Globalization may be enabling people around the world to choose from a wider basket of goods for their economic needs, but it is not turning everyone into the same people. It is not blurring the edges of ethnic identities. Primordialist contributions clearly demonstrate that ethnic identities do not easily disappear.

YOU DECIDE

Which type of primordialism do you find most convincing and why? Is there a component of our ethnic makeup which is genetic? What does this mean in terms of identity?

Is ethnocentrism, or the definition of in-group and out-group, always dangerous to the out-group? Is it anywhere benign?

Bibliography

Albert, M., and Obler, L. (1978) *The Bilingual Brain*. New York: Academic Press.

Connor, W. (1994) *Ethnonationalism*. Princeton, NJ: Princeton University Press.

Durbin, E.F.M. and Bowlby, J. (1938) 'Personal Aggressiveness and War', in *War and Democracy*, edited by E. F. M. Durbin and G. Catlin. London: Kegan Paul.

Geertz, C. (1963) 'Primordial Sentiments and Civil Politics in the New States', in *Old Societies and New States*, edited by C. Geertz. New York: The Free Press of Glencoe.

Huntington, S. (1998) *Clash of Civilizations*. New York: Touchstone Books.

Kellas, J.G. (1998) *The Politics of Nationalism and Ethnicity*. Second ed. New York: St. Martin's Press.

Laponce, J.A. (1985) 'Protecting the French Language in Canada', *Journal of Commonwealth and Comparative Politics* 23:157–70.

Reynolds, Vernon, Falger and Vine. (1987) *The Sociobiology of Ethnocentrism*. Athens, Georgia: The University of Georgia Press.

Shils, E. (1996) *The Torment of Secrecy: The Background and Consequences of American Security Policies*. Chicago: Ivan R. Dee Publisher.

Smith, A.D. (1986) *The Ethnic Origins of Nations*. New York: Basil Blackwell.

Tsunoda, T. (1978) *The Japanese Brain*. Tokyo: Taishukan.

Tylor, E.B. (1871) *Primitive Culture*. London: Murray.

van den Berghe, P.L. (1981) *The Ethnic Phenomenon*. New York: Elsevier.

CHAPTER 3

Instrumentalism

Ethnicity. . . entails not the collective will to exist but the existing will to collect.

[Horowitz 1985]

Instrumentalists view ethnicity as the means to some specific political end, and as such it is focused on the goals of ethnic groups rather than the origins. Instrumentalists believe ethnicity is changeable. It is *not* a characteristic acquired at birth and consistent over time. Moreover, instrumentalists believe that ethnic identities may be important at some times and in some circumstances and completely absent at other times.

The Rwandan Genocide

When Rwanda became independent in 1962, power was supposed to change hands from the Belgium colonial administration to the hands of an indigenous government composed mostly of Hutus, the group that comprised the majority of the population. This peaceful transfer of power was blocked by the minority Tutsi groups in the Rwandan population (about 15 per cent) who wanted to retain control of positions they had long held under the colonial administration as the favoured ethnic group. Civil war broke out, forcing many Tutsis to flee the country into neighbouring Congo and Uganda as refugees. The Hutu took over the government and remained in power until 1994, challenged by armed Tutsi opposition movements from the early 1990s forward. Violence broke out between Hutus and Tutsis in 1973, when Tutsis were expelled from universities and public jobs because they exceeded ethnic quotas which had been set. As a result of the restrictive quotas and the violence more Tutsi left Rwanda. In 1994, the Hutu people, led by members of the media and their own local governments, killed 800,000 Tutsi Rwandans and moderate Hutus over 100 days; most of the killing was done with machetes in local communities by community members. The Hutus were led into the genocidal violence by a desire to retain power and control of Rwanda.

What possible motivation would the Hutus have had to engage in such abominable and heinous behaviour towards their neighbours? Could it have been the desire to put the Hutus in a more advantageous position regarding long-term control of the government? Was this narrowly defined self-interest sufficient to mobilize a population to act in a manner so immoral and condemned throughout the world? Some would argue that the behaviour of the Hutus illustrates the instrumentalist theory of ethnicity. Instrumentalism is a belief that ethnic identities develop and nationalism ensues in the pursuit of particular political goals.

The primordialist perspective discussed in the last chapter focuses on the durability of ethnic ties. Even though there are primordialists who believe that the defining quality of ethnic groups is genetic, linguistic or cultural, we group them because of their shared belief in the enduring nature of these ties. In this chapter and the next, we will consider theoretical approaches to ethnicity that have as a central belief the malleability, or changeable nature, of ethnic sentiment. Instrumentalism and social constructivism (Chapter Four) both approach ethnicity as a product of circumstances and individual decisions. However, instrumentalists typically analyze the ways in which ethnicity is manipulated and used by elites to achieve political goals or some form of political mobilization, while social constructivism is far more concerned with the emergence and disappearance of ethnic groups and movements. Therefore, the two categories are closely related and at times collapse into one another.

While instrumentalists acknowledge the importance of objective markers of ethnicity such as symbols, customs, language or even appearance, for most it is behaviour rather than appearance that defines ethnic groups. In other words, it is possible to tell a person's ethnic identity by examining his or her actions and choices. From an instrumentalist perspective, ethnic identities are very similar to social class. They are both forms of social organization that can change over time. Like classes, ethnic groups can join together in the political pursuit of their group interests. We can also think of class identities as being important in some circumstances but completely absent from others. For example, often there is an effort to mobilize class identification during national elections in an attempt to garner support for a candidate. When Bill Clinton first ran for president in 1992, his opponent, George H.W. Bush, came from a well-to-do East Coast oil family. The Clinton campaign promoted Bill Clinton as a self-made man, someone who grew up in a working class family and succeeded without the privileges of a wealthy upbringing. The emphasis on these characteristics of the candidate, rather than the fact that he went to Yale Law School and was a Rhodes Scholar, were meant to promote the popularity of Clinton with working-class voters who would not be able to identify with the prestige of George Bush's family. This strategy proved successful and in some way contributed to his electoral victory in 1992. However, it wasn't a card he could play with every opponent. Issues of class virtually disappeared in the 1996 presidential election when Clinton faced Bob Dole, a decorated WWII veteran. In one campaign, class was an issue; in the next it disappeared entirely. Did the people in America lose all class affiliation in the interim? Of course not, it was simply mobilized as a political issue by elites (and spin doctors) in the first election and not the second. Instrumentalist theories of ethnicity posit that ethnic identities are similar; sometimes ethnic identities are important, either because of circumstances or the role of elites in manipulating identity. Instrumentalists believe that at other times ethnic identities just disappear because they are no longer serving some specific purpose.

THE POLITICAL NATURE OF ETHNICITY

Primordialists believe that ethnicity is deeply rooted in a person's identity because it is somehow fundamental; however, they disagree on what makes it fundamental: biology, culture or myth. Instrumentalists reject this idea altogether and do not believe that ethnicity is a given at all. Instrumentalists argue that ethnicity is both pervasive and deeply rooted because it is politically useful. Ethnic identity has very practical uses just as class identity can have particular political uses. When we see individuals and groups claiming an ethnic affiliation we should ask ourselves the question – 'What are they trying to gain? What is the group or individual trying to achieve?' Building on the class example given above, when a candidate for political office claims to be of a specific ethnic group, instrumentalists might see that as an attempt to obtain the political support – both votes and donations – of the members of that ethnic group.

   One of the best examples of the usefulness of ethnic identities is suggested by Abner Cohen in his study of Hausa traders in Nigeria (Cohen, 1969). Cohen noted that during the colonial era it was possible for the Hausa to get special treatment from the colonial rulers on the basis of their separateness and distinctiveness from other Nigerians. Hausa tended to isolate themselves in particular quarters within cities so that they could socialize and do business with one another. Originally, this isolation within cities dominated by other ethnic groups such as the Yoruba was implemented to allow the Hausa to live in an area which was exclusively Islamic. These Hausa areas became centres for cattle trading and allowed the Hausa to monopolize the cattle trade within Nigeria. Hausa distinctiveness was critical in maintaining a Hausa monopoly on the cattle trade. However, as more and more Yoruba became Muslims the Hausa were no longer a distinct religious group (Cohen, 1969: 13). In spite of the fact that they were increasingly in the religious majority, they still maintained that they were different from other Nigerians. 'Our customs are different; we are Hausa' was the argument used by the Hausa and accepted by the British colonial government (Cohen, 1969: 22).

When independence swept through the African continent in the early 1960s, Nigeria willingly took control of its government away from the British colonial administration. Not everyone benefited from independence however. The Hausa traders were no longer viewed by the Nigerian government as distinctive and were no longer given special privileges. The Nigerian government viewed the Hausa traders as Nigerian, just like everybody else, disregarding their claim to special status. As a result of this new attitude on the part of the political authorities, the Hausa traders converted en masse from Sunni Islam to membership in a Sufi sect called Tijaniyya. One of the fundamental precepts of Tijaniyya Islam is communal prayer. Unlike other forms of Islam in which a believer can pray anywhere as long as he or she faces Mecca, in Tijaniyya Islam the preference is for prayer with one's teacher at least once a day. This necessitated a proximity in living that, once again, justified a separate Hausa Quarter. Based on the beliefs of Tijaniyya Islam the Hausa reclaimed a distinctive identity from other Muslims in Nigeria, this time on the basis of religion rather than ethnicity. Cohen concluded that 'Ethnicity is a fundamentally political phenomenon' (Cohen, 1969) rather than something biological, cultural or linguistic.

Cohen's description of the use of ethnicity in the context of Nigeria is helpful because it gives an example of the way that ethnicity can be both selected and manipulated to achieve a political or an economic end. Ethnicity is never neutral from an instrumentalist point of view. It is used in the political struggle for power as groups pursue their own interests. Individuals can use ethnicity to achieve personal goals, particularly if they are in positions of leadership. Leaders use ethnic identities and sentiment to control a whole group in the attempt to meet their own personal goals. Typically, this happens through the use of symbols that are held to be important to a particular group. A good example of the use of symbol by elites to spur ethnic identification and, ultimately, to mobilize people to violent action was that of the Nazi party in Germany in the early 1930s and through the Second World War. The presence of the flag, the swastika and the large numbers of German people at Nazi party events were all instances of the use of symbols to draw people together for a cause, an attempt to reach them emotionally in order to pull them on board a political agenda. Ethnicity, from this point of view, is not inherently conflictual or political. It must be stirred up by leaders and directed towards a particular goal. It is a tool.

INDIVIDUAL ADVANTAGE

An instrumentalist view of ethnicity emphasizes the advantage that an individual gains from affiliation with a particular ethnic group. In other words, it is self-interest that motivates ethnic identification, and ultimately nationalism. We can think about self-interest as being different from individual to individual depending on what they stand to gain from their ethnic identification. For example, a Puerto Rican running for a post as an alderman in New York City might find it is in her self-interest to emphasize her Puerto Rican identity because of the votes she will receive based on her ethnicity. A Puerto Rican living in suburban Illinois might have some self-interest in identifying as a Puerto Rican because of the support he will receive from the local Puerto Rican community. Both people in these examples are gaining from their identities, but in the first case the reward is far greater and more tangible than in the second. The New York City alderman gains political power and economic benefit (a job) from her identity ties while the Puerto Rican in suburbia gains social benefits. We can think of the benefits of ethnicity as falling into several categories: social, political and economic.

To further illustrate the way instrumentalists think of ethnicity I would like to tell you about my neighbours, Mary and Ameil. Mary and Ameil are Lebanese-Americans and they take great pride in their heritage. Mary is an amazing cook and is always sending over samples of her Lebanese cookies, tabouli and dolmas because she knows how much I like them. They socialize with other Lebanese-Americans in the community and they go to church at the local Maronite Catholic congregation where the priest speaks Arabic as well as English. Mary and Ameil have strong family and cultural ties to their church and to the local Lebanese community. These are social goods, the values of which are hard to measure. Mary and Ameil also receive other benefits from their ethnic identity. The Lebanese community in town is heavily engaged in business and their family gatherings look a lot like chamber of commerce meetings. They own a business that is widely patronized by the Lebanese community as well as many other people in town. When one of the professors from my university ran for local office I put a campaign sign up in my yard. The next day a campaign sign for the opposing candidate went up in Mary and Ameil's yard. Mary came over and explained to me that normally she would vote for the professor since he was of the 'right party', but she was voting for the opposing candidate because the opposing candidate was Lebanese, and it was a family thing.

A primoridalist would argue that Mary and Ameil are just expressing their natural ethnic identities in a variety of ways in their community. An instrumentalist would look at Mary and Ameil and identify the clear economic and political benefits that they and other members of the Lebanese community in my town receive and argue that they choose to identify themselves as Lebanese because of these benefits. An instrumentalist would argue that they calculate the benefit to themselves and identify with the group only if the personal benefits outweigh the costs. It is the protection of common interests rather than the primordial ties of language or culture that hold groups together.

The example of Mary and Ameil is also instructive in a couple of ways. First, it is benign. It is highly unlikely that the Lebanese community in my small town will become mobilized to challenge the state. Second, it is clear that Mary and Ameil have to give something up in order to be a part of the Lebanese community. They have to give up their time in order to participate in their church, in Lebanese community groups and in the annual Lebanese festival. One might argue that they are sacrificing for, or purchasing their membership in this community group. If we were to ask Mary and Ameil, they would reply that they are happy to make these sacrifices or payments in order to be part of the group. They receive benefits from their participation in the community that make their contributions worthwhile.

If Mary and Ameil present a benign example of ethnicity, we can identify other examples of ethnic identification that are substantially less so. For example, in Northern Ireland, young people can decide whether to join paramilitary groups of their particular religious group, Protestant or Catholic. Why might young people join a paramilitary group? What benefits do they receive? In this case, as in a few others around the globe where young people have grown up in a culture of violence, they may extract benefits such as a sense of direction and revenge from membership in a paramilitary group. We may not view these to be positive reasons for joining a paramilitary group, but growing up in a culture of violence – whether it be Northern Ireland, the West Bank or inner city Chicago – molds the goals and aspirations of young people, sometimes in a negative way. Once a young person joins one of these paramilitary groups he must obey the commands he is given, adhere to the rules and requirements of the group and willingly sacrifice his exit option. You cannot join a paramilitary group and then a few months later decide you do not want to be in it anymore. That type of freedom of decision is not allowed in an organization in which secrecy is vital.

Michael Hechter (2000) has argued that individuals willingly give up certain freedoms to organizations in order to secure wealth, power and prestige. He claims that affiliation with a nation is one way to achieve power and influence. While a paramilitary group may appear to be an extreme example of Hechter's idea, it seems less extreme when compared with the ethnic violence that occurred in Rwanda when genocide was committed in the name of ethnic power.

A group exists to achieve particular goals, rather than simply existing. This is a fine distinction, yet one which separates the primordialists from the instrumentalists. Instrumentalists believe that the ethnic group has particular political goals and that these goals lead to ethnic identities and the development of organizations that exist to pursue the good of the group. Primordialists would argue that the ethnic identities simply exist and that ethnically based organizations exist as a result.

The book *Beyond the Melting Pot*, examines the ethnic identities and organizations of New York Jews, Irish, African-Americans and Puerto Ricans. Examining the strength of ethnic ties for these groups, authors Glazer and Moynihan have noted that it is not necessarily the case that the presence of people of various ethnicities leads to ethnic identification. 'Social and political institutions do not merely respond to ethnic interests; a great number of institutions exist for the specific purpose of serving ethnic interests. This in turn tends to perpetuate them' (Glazer and Moynihan, 1963).

We can take this analysis one step further and argue that ethnic groups exist not because they are somehow organic or biological, but because they provide some benefit to their members. For instrumentalists that benefit is conceived of as political. Social constructivists, as we will see in the next chapter, are a bit freer about the types of benefits that can lead an individual to seek identification with a particular ethnic group.

LEADERSHIP

Instrumentalists see ethnic identity as a path to some sort of political benefit. It is not surprising, therefore, that instrumentalists have focused on the role of leadership in mobilizing people toward ethnic identification and then onward to a political goal. Leadership is fundamental to every political movement. Because ethnic identities typically encompass large numbers of people, the potential leadership pool for ethnic movements is large. Esman has noted that ethnic movements in the Western world have had the support of a large number of well-educated people whose expectations of success and power have not been met under the status quo (Esman, 1977). These educated individuals provide leadership and become an alternative elite that can challenge the state and other ethnic groups.

Paul Brass (Brass, 1991) has studied the leadership role played by elites with regard to ethnicity. His work is based primarily on Indian politics. In India there are a wide variety of ethnic, linguistic and religious groups, the abundance of which leads to complex personal identity issues for each citizen. Brass has noted that ethnic identities in such a complex society are fluid and often conflictual. His work in India has led him to conclude that elites can both create ethnic groups and transform them. Elites of various ethnic groups manipulate ethnic sentiment to take advantage of some economic or political opportunity that may exist. Another example of this would be the sudden politicization of ethnicity throughout the former Yugoslavia as the Soviet Union collapsed, which is detailed in Chapter Six. Brass argues further that ethnic conflict and nationalist demands can only take place in an environment where there is conflict between elites within the country. These elites might be ethnic or religious. He has argued that conflicts within a state can occur when there is disagreement between competing religious elites from different ethnic groups or when there is conflict between religious and ethnic elites. Clearly, this is a model of ethnic conflict that is developed in a context of multiple religious groups and multiple ethnic groups. However, Brass's point can be applied more generally, elites within particular groups will pursue goals which are viewed to benefit their ethnic or religious group.

Ethnic groups are convenient for mobilizing people politically in the pursuit of the goals of particular groups of elites. Ethnicity resonates with most people and therefore it is a very powerful tool in the creation of incentives for political action. However, the people seeking to mobilize ethnic groups in this way often have their own political agendas to promote. They do not always represent the interests of the particular ethnic group in question, but instead their own best interests. Self-aggrandizement or the pursuit of personal power govern their efforts to get people to act in the name of a particular ethnic group.

An excellent and often cited example of the role of an individual leader in ethnic conflict is that of Slobodan Milosevic in Yugoslavia. When the Soviet Union collapsed and Yugoslavia was left to its own devices, there was an internal scramble for power and influence. Slobodan Milosevic was well prepared for this power struggle as he had been championing the cause of the Serbian people in Yugoslavia since the late 1980s. Milosevic made himself a leader among the Serbs in 1987 when he delivered a speech to Serbs living in Kosovo. It was intended that Milosevic would pacify the Serbs regarding their relationship with the Kosovar Albanians, but rather than doing that, Milosevic promised the Serbs in Kosovo that the Albanian police would never be able to 'beat' them again. This whipped up Serbian ethnic sentiment all through Kosovo and Yugoslavia as it was televised throughout the country. Many would argue that Milosevic manipulated Serbian nationalist sentiment in an effort to gain power for himself personally. To the extent that this is true, it fits well with the instrumentalist view of ethnicity.

Milosevic's role in fomenting ethnic conflict will be examined in Chapter Six where the conflicts in the former Yugoslavia are discussed in more detail. What is particularly notable about Milosevic, and important as an example here, is the fact that an individual was so influential in defining an ethnic group and identifying a collective goal for that group.

The case of Milosevic is just one example of the influential role that leaders can play both in rhetoric and in defining the boundaries of who belongs to a group and who does not. Milosevic's speech clearly identified an 'us' – the Serbs, and a 'them' – the Kosovar Albanians. Prior to Milosevic's speech there had not been strong Serbian ethnic sentiment. It began to develop as Serbian interests were defined and the boundaries of the group of belonging were firmly established.

	Primordialist	*Instrumentalist*
Origins of identity	Innate and ancient	Manipulated and variable over time
Goals of ethnic groups	Undefined	Political and economic gain
Role of leaders	Undefined	Critical in defining goals
Ethnicity attribute of	Group	Individual
Ethnicity viewed as conflictual or neutral	Conflictual	Conflictual
Expiration of identities		Can disappear when no longer politically expedient

DEFINING THE OTHER

Readers who have gotten this far in the text will by now understand that ethnicity is all about personal identity and establishing a group with whom one feels emotionally tied. In this chapter and the next, we see a flexible approach to ethnicity that allows some freedom for individual choice in ethnic identification and selection. This will be raised in greater detail in the next chapter, when we discuss social constructivism and the importance of individual choice in the birth, formation and disappearance of ethnic groups. However, it is important to touch on the issue very briefly in this chapter as well, not because of the importance of the individual in choosing affiliation with a particular group, but rather because of the use of ethnicity in defining 'the other'.

An ethnic identity can be applied to a group of people who would not necessarily choose that identity. Defining the other is a political strategy and it is an instrumental use of ethnic identity. Typically, the 'other' group is cast in a negative light. Fredrik Barth, in a famous study of ethnicity entitled *Ethnic Groups and Boundaries*, has argued that identity is primarily concerned with constructing the boundaries between groups. It is just as important to define who one *is not* as it is to define who one *is*. Barth argues that some ethnic identities are not chosen by an individual but imposed upon that person by others (Barth, 1998). Perhaps the best example of this type of imposition of identity exists in the instances of genocide which we have witnessed in the twentieth century. The Nazi regime in Germany was extremely concerned with classifying people according to their ethnicity, which they defined by both religion and descent. This classification was used to select those who would be killed. The reasons why the Nazi regime did this ultimately boil down to two issues: 1) the narrow nationalism and racism of the regime that defined itself in opposition to Jews, as well as Gypsies and others that were considered 'undesirable', and 2) the need to find someone to blame for the post-World War I economic devastation that impoverished so many Germans. During the Nazi era, Jews were defined in the widest sense possible. The Germans defined Jews not only as those practicing or identifying with the faith or the people, but also with those of other faiths or who considered themselves atheists but who happened to have a small percentage of 'Jewish' blood. Having one Jewish grandparent was enough to justify being sent to the death camps. Additionally, the Germans attributed certain physical characteristics to the Jews and distinctly different characteristics to themselves. The capriciousness of this type of physical characterization is typified by a scene in the movie, *Europa, Europa,* in which a schoolteacher singles out a young Jewish boy as a perfect example of Aryan physical type.

In 1994, genocide occurred in Rwanda when the majority Hutu population killed most of the Tutsi population of the country in a period of about two months. There are many stories from this genocide of Tutsis surviving because they were thought to be Hutu. Ethnic identity in Rwanda seems to have been determined in a fairly arbitrary way at the end of the nineteenth century and beginning of the twentieth century, prior to the genocide. The delineation between who was Hutu and who was Tutsi was not absolutely clear. However, under the colonial administration of the Belgians, people were assigned to an ethnic group and they were forced to carry identity cards noting their group as a means of facilitating administration by the state. Historically, the Tutsi are believed to have emigrated to Rwanda – perhaps from Ethiopia – and they assumed rule over the Hutu in many areas, though not all of the country. When the Germans and then the Belgians took over the territory of Rwanda, they assumed a policy of indirect rule and chose to administer the colony through the Tutsi aristocracy (Prunier, 1995). The colonial government demonstrated a preference for the employment and education of Tutsis. Thus, at the time of independence there were more Tutsis who were educated, in government, and in positions of authority, than Hutus, in spite of the fact that Tutsis were a minority of the population. The boundaries that had been established between the Hutu and Tutsi ethnic groups under the colonial administration became politicized under the administration of the independent Rwandan state. Ultimately, the result of the politicization of these ethnic boundaries was genocide. The colonial state firmly established the boundaries between ethnic groups and labeled each one. Individuals in Rwanda were not allowed to choose an ethnic identity – one was assigned to them.

In these two examples where genocide occurred, we see the role of the state in defining the boundaries between ethnic groups in order to achieve some political end. In Nazi Germany the political goal was to cast blame for an economic crisis and promote the Aryan ethnic group. In the case of Rwanda, the reasons were far more mundane. Ethnic groups were defined in order to rule the Rwandan population. In both cases ethnicity was attributed to groups of people rather than chosen by individuals. It is no accident that the role of the state in assigning ethnicity to particular groups coincided with state violence against those groups. In many of the cases in which we find ethnicity being assigned to others the reasons for doing so are not altruistic or even ambivalent.

Enemy Images

In the relations between and within states we see many examples of the use of media and imagery to define or portray a particular group of people or a country in a negative way. This construction of enemy images is one way in which both countries and individuals can define the 'other'. We see an example of this is in the rhetoric of the US President in the wake of the September 11, 2001, attacks on the World Trade Centre and the Pentagon. George W. Bush referred to those who had conducted the attacks in the following way.

> We are not deceived by their pretenses to piety. We have seen their kind before. They are the heirs of all the murderous ideologies of the 20th century. By sacrificing human life to serve their radical visions – by abandoning every value except the will to power – they follow in the path of fascism, and Nazism, and totalitarianism. And they will follow that path all the way, to where it ends: in history's unmarked grave of discarded lies. (Bush, 2001)

In using these strong images associating the attackers with Nazism, fascism, lies and murder as well as questioning their religious faith, George W. Bush draws a clear boundary between those who attacked the US and anything positive or justifiable. In so doing he is creating images of the enemy, defining them in a particular way and at the same time creating a justification for US action in response to the attack. This is an example of how a state can use enemy images to define a country or a people in a negative light. It is one example of the way that a state can use emotional or psychological ties to promote its own interests.

THE INSTRUMENTAL STATE

We can press this understanding of instrumentalism still further and discuss the role of the state in mobilizing nationalism. If, from an instrumental perspective the goal of nationalism is always to achieve some political end, then nationalism should be nowhere as evident as in the political actions of states. Indeed, we do find the presence and manipulation of ethnic identities within the state, or more precisely, within effective states. An effective state is one that is able to encourage nationalist sentiment within its population. A state that is able to manipulate ethnic identities in its own interests is able to combat the development and strength of sub-state ethnic identities.

Nationalist sentiment in support of the state – what we might otherwise call civic nationalism – is tremendously important for the well-being of the state. States do not pursue this strategy either because they choose not to, or because they cannot. Whatever is the reason, states that do not make an effort to promote civic nationalism are ultimately weaker.

Why do states need nationalism?

Recall the original definition of nationalism given in the introduction: it is an emotional or a psychological attachment to a group, a shared fundamental identity. When we discuss nationalism in support of the state, or civic nationalism, the group to which that psychological or emotional attachment applies includes all citizens of a particular country. It seems obvious that a state needs the support of its citizens in order to rule. However, the nature by which a state gains this support is instructive. States can maintain the compliance of their citizens either through the threat of force or through voluntary cooperation. Since the first option is far more expensive than the second, it is better for all parties if voluntary cooperation occurs. One way to obtain voluntary cooperation from citizens is to encourage a psychological or emotional attachment to the state. This attachment instils a sense of obligation in the population, to the point where obeying laws becomes not what one must do, but what one ought to do. For example, I know that I ought to pay my taxes because I receive many services from the state. Therefore, I pay my taxes, not necessarily because I am afraid of being audited and receiving a penalty of some sort, but because I feel a sense of obligation to do so. Once a sense of obligation is developed, the resources the state must devote to enforcing the compliance of the citizenry to laws decrease markedly. There are several ways of looking at the state's use of nationalism to pursue its own goals. We will begin here by examining the most obvious cases first – the use of nationalism in times of war – and then how nationalism is invoked and manipulated during times of peace to promote the well-being of the state.

Nationalism in times of war

At no time is the necessity for an emotional attachment to the state more pronounced and more manipulated than in times of war. The support of the citizenry in times of war is absolutely vital. It is critical that citizens understand the threat to the state and the possible shortages and deprivations that they may experience as a result of the government's response to the threat. Though this has become less obvious in the current era of high-tech warfare in the West, there are some clear examples. During the First Gulf War rising gas prices were a cost that had to be paid by citizens throughout Europe and North America. These costs were a direct result of the military action but the government was not blamed or threatened by the temporary increase in the cost of gasoline. This type of civilian deprivation as a result of war is miniscule compared to the effects on the average citizen during the Second World War. During that war, citizens on the home front were subject to rationing of sugar, meat, cigarettes, gasoline, clothing and more. They held scrap metal and blood drives to support the troops in the field. Moreover, for citizens of European nations, the war was fought on their land, in their homes and in the skies above them. Their sacrifices were tremendous and these sacrifices were willingly made in support of the state. Popular patriotic slogans during the Second World War urged citizens to support their country.

If you can't go – buy war bonds : Our bonds are their security!!

Ride together – work together – save rubber for victory.

I pledge allegiance and silence about the war.

The emotional attachment and popular support of the state gave meaning to wartime sacrifices during the Second World War.

Patriotic sentiment is even more important among the young people who make up a country's fighting force. If a government wants young men and women to volunteer for the armed services and put their lives on the line in battle for the state, then nationalism becomes a necessity. It is needed for a particular political end – the security of the state, the defense of the nation. Jean Bethke Elshtain noted that in the past century it was a 'will-to-sacrifice' in order to defend their homeland that led young people to volunteer for the armed services rather than a deep hatred of the enemy and a desire to kill them (Elshtain, 1993). Nationalism is also important among those who are drafted, since, even if one would not choose military service of one's own free will, a love of country and emotional attachment to its citizenry will elicit better performance from soldiers once they are drafted.

A high level of patriotic sentiment means that the country will be better able to stomach the deaths of soldiers than if that sentiment was absent or weak. Thus, the use of nationalist rhetoric to incite civic nationalism has a specific political goal. We can consider it to be a form of instrumentalism because nationalism is used for the political end of supporting the actions of the particular government in power in response to the needs that they face in times of great crisis. It is certainly a smaller subset of instrumentalism as a whole, but it is nonetheless a use of ethnicity, very broadly construed, for political ends. Moreover, the more effective a state is the more it will be able to use nationalism in order to combat sub-state allegiances and encourage the overall cooperation of the populace.

Not only does nationalist rhetoric inspire people to make great sacrifices for their country, it is also used by governments to justify their actions in international conflicts or in response to security threats. Governments around the world use nationalist rhetoric to encourage their citizenry to support the cause of the state; indeed, as argued earlier, the most effective states are those that can actually motivate people to some sort of action or sentiment based on their manipulation of nationalism.

PEACETIME NATIONALISM

It is the day to day manipulation of nationalism that is important for strengthening the state in times of peace as well as times of war. Michael Billig refers to the peaceful daily production and reproduction of nationalism in the West as 'banal nationalism' (Billig, 1995). He refers to it as banal nationalism because it is the mundane and repetitive emphasis on citizenship and the state, the 'constant drum' of nationalism, that encourages identification with the state as opposed to some other sub-state group. Most of this type of everyday nationalism, while pervasive, passes us by without much fanfare and is thus easily overlooked.

As an example, in every country images of the flag serve to reinforce nationalist sentiment, even if there is nothing particularly notable about the image. Thus, an image of the Union Jack on a packet of shortbread biscuits is not in any way remarkable in the UK. Yet, it does promote nationalism at some level (and perhaps also the association of nationalism with something sweet). The presence of flags in churches throughout North America and the United Kingdom also reinforces nationalist sentiment and a strong association of nationalism with God. Images associated with the state abound in our daily lives. It is a good exercise to begin to note when you see nationalist images and why they are there. These images of the flag, the queen, the statue of liberty and other symbols of the state are emphasized by shared rituals revolving around national holidays and sporting activities. If you are American, it seems natural to spend the Fourth of July barbequing and watching fireworks displays. Similarly if you are a citizen of the United Kingdom you may have a tradition of watching the Queen's speech each Christmas Day. These holidays offer opportunities to engage in ritualized behaviour which reinforces nationalist sentiment.

More overt displays of nationalism are ritualized at sporting events, such as the Olympics, where the winner of a gold medal has his or her anthem played at the awards ceremony. It is interesting to note the number of athletes who, after achieving great personal success, weep as their national anthem is played. There is, in this ceremony, a great conflation of emotion, personal success and tenderness towards the motherland. Watching the Olympics on television and cheering for your particular national team reinforces an attachment to your state. A more mundane exhibit of ritualized nationalism occurs daily in the United States as students in virtually every school across the country begin their day by pledging allegiance to the flag.

These peacetime manifestations of nationalism all serve the political interests of the state. The more patriotic we all feel, the more likely we are to pay our taxes without complaining, obey the laws and even volunteer to serve in the armed forces. The less patriotic we are, and the less patriotic those around us are, the less we will feel inclined to act in ways that support the state without being coerced into doing so.

How does a state promote national identity?

Since the citizenry of a state is a wide and varied group, no matter what the country, it takes some involvement on the part of the government to get people to identify their own personal interests with the interests of all citizens of the state. Early attempts at socialization, such as getting all youngsters to pledge allegiance to the flag, is one effective way of encouraging an acceptance of national identity. The use of flags and other symbols also ensures a mundane reinforcement of nationalism.

Yet states can and do go further in promoting nationalist sentiment. States create legal holidays in which people are given a day off of work to remember the state. In the US this is most obviously Independence Day. In the United Kingdom, Remembrance Day, November 11, serves a similar function by bringing all citizens of the state together to honour the memories of those who died in war. Implicit in this remembering is not just the memory of the people who died, but the cause that they viewed worthy of sacrificing their lives – loyalty to the state. These sentiments are reinforced further by the presence of the royal family and the prime minister, and their solemnity as they lay poppy wreaths at the cenotaph. These rituals reinforce a feeling of national identity.

Civic nationalism, or nationalism in support of the state, is an attempt both to strengthen the state and to weaken competing sub-state nationalisms. In other words, we can view civic nationalism as an attempt to overcome ethnic nationalism. Thus, we expect that over time new immigrants will no longer see themselves as Russians who have come to the United States, or as naturalized Koreans, but simply as Americans. Civic nationalism promotes the homogenizing action of 'the melting pot'. It creates shared values and rituals among people who have little in common otherwise. Creating shared values within a state – what Ernst Haas refers to as *rationalization* (Haas, 1997) – creates states that are viewed as legitimate by their populations. Where you have a common view of the legitimacy of the state you are far less likely to see any sort of internal ethnic conflict and unlikely to see an ethnic group rise up to challenge the state.

As reinforcing civic nationalism, or a sense of emotional attachment to the state has so many positive benefits, why don't all states engage in this sort of behaviour in order to strengthen the state? Part of the reason may be that the state is unable to do so, either because it has few resources or because it is already embattled in some sort of civil strife. It is very difficult for a state that is engaged in active conflict with a segment of its population to try and develop emotional attachments to the state among that group. You can imagine how any attempt to promote the Union of the United States of America would have been received in the South, either immediately before, during, or immediately after the civil war. It would have been quite ineffective. The state was already divided and attempts to promote civic nationalism would have been equally ineffective.

A second reason why states might not use nationalism in this instrumental way is because the state is already in the hands of a particular ethnic group and its goal is the domination, rather than the integration, of other ethnic groups. Liberia, prior to the outbreak of its civil war in 1989, was an example of this type of state. The Krahn people dominated the government and the armed forces, and there was no effort and apparently no desire to effectively integrate other ethnic groups into the state apparatus or even into a support of the state that the Krahn controlled. It is not surprising then that the Liberian state was weak and eventually collapsed, though there were certainly other factors at play as well.

The instrumental use of nationalism by the state is critical to ensuring state strength. The strongest states are those that are able to use nationalism to tie the sentiments of their citizenry to support for the values and goals of the state. States are able to manipulate nationalist feelings through a variety of methods including the use of symbols, songs, rituals and traditions. Those states that neglect to manipulate nationalism are necessarily weaker and often lacking in support or legitimacy.

CRITICISMS OF INSTRUMENTALISM

Instrumentalism has become a part of the scholarly consensus regarding understanding ethnic identity and nationalism. However, criticisms of the instrumentalist approach remain, several of which come from the primordialist point of view that ethnic identities are rooted in more than simply personal or political gain.

Those who support an instrumentalist approach to ethnicity fall into one of two camps. They believe either 1) that ethnic identification is merely the manifestation of other more fundamental political or economic conflicts, or 2) that ethnicity is a kind of external identity that is promoted within particular groups by elites with political or personal agendas of their own. Any sort of view of nationalism as used by the state would fall under this second category.

Yet ethnicity still proves to be a problem for instrumentalists in that they have difficulty understanding ethnic affiliations on their own that seem to exist without some wider political purpose or goal either for the particular individual or for elites of that ethnic group. It is illustrative to return to the example of Ameil and Mary, my Lebanese neighbours that began the chapter. If Ameil and Mary received no political benefits from identifying themselves as Lebanese, then instrumentalism could not explain their ethnic affiliation. A feeling of belonging in and of itself would not be sufficient for ethnic identity from an instrumentalist perspective. Yet, people often state that they hold a particular ethnic identification because it gives them a sense of belonging or because it is simply inherent to their own identity. These explanations are inconsistent with the instrumentalist perspective which sees ethnic identity as contingent upon political goals and political agendas.

Instrumentalists also have great difficulty explaining the persistence of ethnic groups across time. Political agendas and goals, whether they are held by elites or by individuals, will shift over time in response to changing economic and political circumstances. Since the political and economic situation within a country is always changing we should see a landscape of consistently shifting ethnic groups and ethnic affiliations. Yet this is not always the case. At times we see a continued adherence to ethnic identification within a particular group, for example among the Welsh over the past two centuries, despite the fact that the economic and political circumstances affecting the incentives to be identified as Welsh have changed greatly. Instrumentalists are able to aptly describe why someone might choose to be Welsh in the current political climate in the United Kingdom where a Welsh identity is valued both politically and culturally. However, it is far less obvious why there were people identifying themselves as Welsh in the 1950s when there seemed little to gain from the identity, as Welsh independence and local governance was not on the political agenda.

The idea that elites are the defining factor in articulating nationalism and ethnic identity can also be challenged. A situation in which leadership arises to respond to and follow the will of the masses is counter to the arguments espoused by instrumentalists. The Eritrean example discussed in Chapter Eight provides an example. Issayas Afeworki, the clear leader of the Eritrean independence movement, did not himself create the movement. He was formed by the movement, and he later transformed the movement, but it existed before he came of age.

YOU DECIDE

Should a state manipulate the emotional sentiments of its population? If so, how much manipulation is appropriate? Is there a line that should not be crossed?
Do leaders form movements or do movements form leaders?
Are leaders who use nationalism to pursue their own goals doing something wrong or unethical?

Bibliography

Barth, F. (1998) *Ethnic Groups and Boundaries*. Prospect Heights, IL: Waveland Press, Inc.

Billig, M. (1995) *Banal Nationalism*. Thousand Oaks, CA: Sage Publications.

Brass, P.R. (1991) *Ethnicity and Nationalism*. Newbury Park: Sage.

Bush, G.W. (2002) *September 20 Address to a Joint Session of Congress and the American People* 2001 (cited January 9, 2002). Available from http://www.whitehouse.gov/news/releases/2001/09/20010920-8.html

Cohen, A. (1969) *Custom and Politics in Urban Africa*. Berkeley, CA: University of California Press.

Elshtain, J.B. (1993) 'Sovereignty, Identity, Sacrifice', in *Reimagining the Nation*, edited by M. Ringrose and A. J. Lerner. Buckingham: Open University Press.

Esman, M. (1977) *Ethnic Conflict in the Western World*. Ithaca, NY: Cornell University Press.

Glazer, N. and Moynihan D.P. (1963) *Beyond the Melting Pot*. Cambridge, Mass: MIT and Harvard University Press.

Haas, E.B. (1997) *Nationalism, Liberalism and Progress*. Ithaca, NY: Cornell University Press.

Hechter, M. (2000) *Containing Nationalism*. New York: Oxford University Press.

Horowitz, D.L. (1985) *Ethnic Groups in Conflict*. Berkeley, CA: University of California Press.

Prunier, G. (1995) *The Rwanda Crisis*. New York: Columbia University Press.

CHAPTER 4

Social Constructivism

...if one looks down the dark ravines of history, one sees that men in social groups need some other group to hate.

[Bell 1975]

Social constructivism is a theoretical school of ethnicity that focuses on the fluid nature of ethnic identities. It is similar to instrumentalism in that it identifies the role of political and economic factors in molding ethnicity. However, social constructivism is different because it addresses the origins of ethnic groups and does not view all ethnic expressions as in some way opportunistic. Social constructivists see language, religion and/or physical characteristics as creating the set of identities from which one can choose, but as inadequate explanations for ethnic identity or national affiliation. People choose an ethnic identity based on their identity set plus their own preferences, which are formed by economic, political and even social conditions.

The Rwandan Genocide

In 1994, 800,000 Tutsis were killed in Rwanda. They were killed by Hutu people who desired to end the dominant role that Tutsis had played in the government and armed forces of Rwanda. Moderate Hutus who opposed the violence or were involved in political alliances with the Tutsis were also killed. The reasons behind the genocide were the struggle for political power coupled with a desire for revenge on the Tutsi who had been favoured in terms of educational opportunities and political leadership during the colonial era. This favoured position of the Tutsi was based on German and Belgian beliefs in the superiority of the generally taller and lighter skinned Tutsi.[1] Thus, in the case of Rwanda the ethnic violence that developed referenced an earlier era in which ethnicity was both constructed and manipulated to divide and conquer the country.

---

[1] Some scholars, such as Lucy Mair, have argued that the ethnic identifications of Hutu and Tutsi are more arbitrary than just appearance. She has argued that these identities were given to Rwandans during the colonial era on the basis of how many cattle they owned (Mair, L., 1974. *African Societies*. New York: Cambridge University Press).

Social constructivism is the dominant view at the beginning of the twenty-first century. It has been theoretically convincing to many scholars because the theory tells us why we see particular ethnic groups develop and why we see some fade from view. Constructivists recognize ethnic identity as a combination of inborn traits and social inputs. For example, since I am white, the chances that I can become Native American are not high. That would not be an identity which I can choose. However, I do have a variety of other possible identities that are not constrained by my appearance. I can make religious choices and linguistic choices. I can move to another country or choose to emphasize one part of my heritage rather than another. Thus, while my choices may not be unlimited, they do exist. When I was growing up in America my parents told me that I was Czech, Irish and German, and I accepted these identifications (even though there was such a variety). After becoming an adult and traveling extensively overseas, I now think of myself as an American rather than anything else. My identity has been constructed by my experiences overseas. I view myself much differently than my parents view themselves. I do not feel a strong association with any ethnic homeland. My identity has been constructed by experiences different from those of my parents and therefore I see myself differently. Constructivists believe that group boundaries are changeable within certain limits.

The Formation of Ethnic Identity

Ascribed traits + social inputs = ethnic identity

Ascribed traits	**Social Inputs**
Appearance	ancestral myths
Place of birth	subjective beliefs
Language	political power of group
	economics
	religion
	language

Language appears in both categories because its role in the formation of ethnic identities is contested. Some would argue that language is an ascribed trait and some think that it can be learned.

Social constructivists argue that ethnicity is 'partly ascribed and partly volitional' (Nagel, 1986). A resident of Calgary is an Albertan in Canada, but a Canadian in the United States. Similarly, a Boran is a Southerner or an Oromo within Ethiopia, an Ethiopian in the rest of

Africa, and an African to the rest of the world. Our ethnic identities can shift over time as the context we are in changes. They can also change in relation to varying economic and political incentives and as the context an individual is in alters. This understanding of the flexible nature of ethnicity is particularly interesting in the Rwandan context.

In Rwanda in 1959, and then again in 1973, many Tutsi fled the country in the wake of ethnic violence. This ethnic violence was nowhere near the scale of the 1994 genocide, but it was significant enough to motivate many Tutsi to leave Rwanda and become refugees in nearby states. Nearly 100,000 Rwandan Tutsi fled to Uganda, where they quickly became involved in politics. These people, who were forced to leave Rwanda because of fear due to their  ethnic identity, lost that identity upon leaving Rwanda and simply became Rwandans (Gourevitch, 1998: 210). Their identity as Rwandans and refugees superceded any specific sub-national identity they had within Rwanda. It was a group of these ethnic Tutsi who had become refugees in Uganda that eventually organized themselves and drove the Hutu responsible for organizing the genocide out of Rwanda and re-established a government there. The irony of these political events illuminates the contextual nature of ethnic identity.

Daniel Bell has argued that the ability to choose between a variety of ethnic identities is a relatively new phenomenon (Bell, 1975). Previously, identities were stipulated by one's clan or tribe or religion. Bell believes that it is only in the modern world with the possibility for rapid social change that identities can be selected in a self-conscious fashion. Bell would argue that the social construction of ethnicity may exist, but it has not always been so. Since social constructivists believe that people can have multiple ascribed identities there is no sense of the predetermined group that exists in primordialism. Social constructivism is distinct from instrument-alism because there is no assumption within social constructivist theory that the group is organized to achieve some sort of group benefit or individual benefit for the leader. Rather, social constructivists are able to envision a variety of reasons as to why people might align themselves with particular ethnic identities and why these identities might become politicized in a form of nationalism.

Thus, the difference between social constructivism and primordi-alism is in the understanding of how ethnic groups form. The distinction between social constructivism and instrumentalism is finer. It relates to the purported political goals of an ethnic group assumed by the instrumentalist approach. The social constructivist views ethnicity to be manufactured rather than innate, but with no needed economic or political goal for it to form.

Imagined identities

One of the most pronounced and direct attacks on the primordialist perspective of the origin of nations has come from historians examining the development of nations and their challenge to states. This has been an interesting problem to unravel from a historical point of view. Benedict Anderson (1991) sees nations as 'imagined communities'. People are included if they think they belong. Benedict argues that such imagined communities only become possible with the advent of modern technologies such as print journalism and are entirely constructed out of the relationships between people. One wonders if newer technologies such as the internet give us even greater power to 'imagine' different kinds of communities in the present era. Anderson's point is that nations are a modern phenomenon, molded by our industrialized world.

GROUP FORMATION AND DISAPPEARANCE

Sociologists have noted that ethnic groups can disappear through assimilation into a larger ethnic group. This is essentially what has happened to many of the white immigrants who came to the United States in the waves of immigration around the turn of the twentieth century. However, while assimilation with a larger group has occurred, the expected outcome of large state-level ethnic groups has not materialized, not in the United States or in any other country, because not every group assimilates. There is a trend of smaller groups assimilating into larger groups, but the state never fully absorbs all ethnic groups; the process is never complete.

It is strange to think of ethnic groups disappearing, so perhaps it is best to use a famous example. In New York City, German immigrants used to have a sizeable and influential ethnic group and organization. Despite the political importance they once had, the Germans as a group have vanished. 'No appeals are made to the German vote, there are no German politicians in the sense that there are Irish or Italian politicians, there are in fact few Germans in political life and, generally speaking, no German component in the structure of the ethnic interests of the city' (Glazer and Moynihan, 1963: 311). How can this be? First there were Germans, and then there were not. As social scientists we want to be able to explain why this might have happened. Part of the explanation lies in the fact that it ceased to be

57

politically correct or popular to be German after the First and Second World Wars. After the Second World War in particular, people who had 'German' in their potential identity set began to choose an alternative identity. Politicians also de-emphasized their German identity when running, never making an explicit attempt to capture the 'German Vote'. Gradually, the German ethnic group simply ceased to exist in New York City. The people of German descent didn't go away, they just 'imagined' or perceived themselves to have a different identity

More commonly, particularly in the post-Cold War era, we see new groups forming. An excellent example is the formation of a Mayan identity in Guatemala. This is such a good example because Latin America is an area which has been thought to be relatively free from a variety of ethnic identifications. Since the end of the Second World War an increasing number of people in Guatemala have been identifying themselves as 'Mayan' rather than Guatemalan or some other ethnic identity. The Mayan movement has developed to promote Mayan unity, culture and languages. Identification as Mayan appears to be the result of several factors. The first was the extension of the franchise in 1945 and the subsequent modernization of the state as that incorporated rural areas and all peoples. Another factor was religion, specifically the 'Catholic Action' movement which was designed to expunge 'unacceptable practices' from Mayan culture and the spread of other religions and ideologies (LeBaron, 1993). This led to the Catholic Church becoming a central player in the revitalization of Mayan ethnicity. Since the late 1970s there is a new Mayan identity that was not previously present. Now politicians run as 'Mayan' candidates. A new political identity has been created.

The Mayan case is a very interesting example of the social construction of ethnicity, because while it was clear that people were Mayan before the revitalization of the identity, being Mayan would not have changed anyone's actions, led anyone to think of themselves as part of a political group, or been the first political identity people would have named if asked.

The remainder of this chapter will be arranged around several categories or usages of social construction theory. First, we will examine the efforts of people to define themselves through the creation of imagined communities. An extreme example of this exists in the development of a myth of chosenness. The second theme that will be developed within the chapter is that of rational action – the idea that people can rationally choose one identity over another and may choose the one that they find most rewarding in a particular political context. The third theme within the theoretical field of social constructivism is the idea that ethnic groups are defined by others and not by themselves. We will examine this theme by looking at some of the sociological theory regarding group formation and then

	Primordialist	Instrumentalist	Social Constructivist
Origins of identity	Innate and ancient	Manipulated and varied in time	A combination of innate characteristics and socially generated myths, modern
Goals of ethnic groups	Undefined	Political and economic gain	Various
Role of leaders	Undefined	Critical in defining goals	
Ethnicity attribute of	Group	Individual	Group
Ethnicity viewed as conflictual or neutral	Conflictual	Conflictual	Neutral
Expiration of identities		Can disappear when no longer politically expedient	Can disappear for a variety of reasons

examining the definition of ethnicity in Los Angeles. The last theme we will consider is competition theory.

THE CONTEXTUAL DEFINITION OF ETHNICITY

It is not what is, *but* what people believe is *that has behavioural consequences.*

[Connor 1994]

As mentioned in the quote above, it is what people believe that molds their actions. The belief that God has set a people apart for a particular mission is an extremely interesting example of the power of beliefs. The myth of the 'chosen people' has distinguished many groups in their own eyes for specific actions or for power. The chosen people imagery is present in a variety of cultures.

'Chosen People' myths

The definitive example of a chosen people is the Jews of the Old Testament. The close relationship that God has with the Jews is described in the first books of the Bible; God's concern with their victory in battle over other people, the establishment of their state and the distinctiveness of the Jewish people in custom and law all set the Jews apart and above other peoples in the account of the Old Testament. Even when the Jews do not follow their God or fail in their duties, they maintain their status as the chosen ones and a certain superiority to those around them.

The Jews are the model for the idea of a chosen race which has since been claimed by many other groups all over the world. The Afrikaners of South Africa, a group of white South Africans, descended from the Dutch, French Huguenot and German settlers in the Cape in the mid 1600s, have based their domination of other people in South Africa, among other factors, on their status as the 'chosen people' of God. The understanding of the 'chosenness' of Afrikaners seems to have developed over time as the Afrikaners faced threats of domination from English settlers within South Africa after the Boer War of 1899 – 1902. After losing that war, and the establishment of South Africa as an English Colony, many Afrikaners travelled inland from the coast to farm land away from the English settlements. This movement inland, called the Great Trek, is memorialized in Afrikaner history as the definitive point in time where God led the chosen people (here Afrikaners) out of the land of Egypt (or British controlled South Africa). Henning Klopper, an Afrikaner of contemporary times, speaks of the perception among Afrikaners of the divinely ordained nature of the Great Trek in David Harrison's book, *The White Tribe of Africa*. Klopper was responsible for organizing a reenactment of the Great Trek 100 years after it occurred. Klopper states:

> Although I organized it and had everything to do with it, I felt it was completely taken out of my hands. The whole feeling of the trek was the working not of man, not of any living being. It was the will and the work of the Almighty God. It was a pilgrimage, a sacred happening. (Harrison, 1981)

A chaplain presiding over the reenactment was more explicit regarding the symbolism of the Trek reenactment and its meaning for the Afrikaner people:

> We have received a fire from God, that fire is our nationhood. It is wonderful to think that this nationhood is from God, a burning torch which is not extinguished. It has been kept burning all the way from the statue of van Riebeeck to here. By the mercy of God it has burned until now. It must be kept burning. (Harrison, 1981)

The Afrikaners used the chosen people myth to justify their own manifest destiny – their claim over the vast territories and peoples of inland South Africa. Believing that your group is chosen by God over other groups to fulfill a particular destiny is a powerful self-definition and has implications for members of other groups that come into conflict with the chosen. Any out-group in conflict with a group that has a chosen people myth faces demonization and attributions of evil simply because they are not the chosen ones. The chosen people myth is both empowering and dangerous. It empowers the people in whom it is articulated and it is extremely dangerous for those who oppose them. Social constructivists would see the development of a myth of chosenness as a response to political or economic circumstances, much in the way they would view the development or diminishment of an ethnic identity.

RATIONAL CHOICES AND ETHNIC IDENTITIES

Why does conflict break out between some groups and not others? Why did violent 'ethnic' conflict develop between the Serbs, Croats and Bosnian Muslims in the former Yugoslavia, but not between the Flemish and Walloons in Belgium? Clearly, ethnicity alone is not a sufficient explanation of nationalist actions. What then will explain it? The rational choice approach to ethnic identity and nationalism uses the tools of rational choice theory coupled with the assumptions of social constructivism to explain what motivates individuals to identify with a particular ethnic group and then to act in a nationalist fashion.

Rational Choice Theory

Rational Choice Theory is an attempt to simplify the way we understand people's actions in such a way as to make those actions more predictable. It uses two critical assumptions to then build a model to predict people's behaviour.

Assumption 1: It is possible to identify people's preferences and goals (either by observing them or asking them).

Assumption 2: All persons are rational maximizers of self-interest. This is rational choice language for saying they look at the options available to them and then, calculating the value of alternative goals, they make a choice in order to obtain what they want.

Rational choice theorists believe that individuals order their preferences and then try to achieve those preferences in a particular order. Typically, when using Rational Choice Theory, the unit of analysis is the individual rather than the group. Therefore, when we use rational choice theory to examine the social construction of ethnicity it is examining what makes an individual choose a particular ethnic identity.

> Rational Choice Theory is an extremely powerful tool. It allows social scientists to attempt to predict behaviour, and in this case it allows them to try and predict people's identity choices.

A rational choice approach to ethnic and political identities would simply argue that people will choose an identity that best suits their own personal interests and goals. This puts the rational choice approach firmly in the constructivist camp for several reasons. First of all, it simply must be the case that a person has a limited set of possible options. If a person were raised in Samoa he would have a difficult time passing himself off as an indigenous Norwegian. However, beyond a somewhat constrained set of identity choices, there are choices that can be made and according to rational choice theorists, these choices will be made in a person's self-interest and in keeping with her goals.

GROUP THEORY

It is very helpful to reference the sociological school of thought called group theory when we address socially constructed ethnic identities and nationalist movements. Group theory addresses two critical aspects of identity: 1) how groups establish their boundaries, and 2) how groups can be formed by opposition. It is helpful here to recall the very simple sociological definition of in-group and out-group. An in-group is a group that an individual feels a part of because of some sort of shared psychological attachment. An out-group is that from which the individual feels distinct or with which a person does not identify. Members of in-groups often have feelings of superiority vis-à-vis other groups, or elevated opinions of themselves and their group. These feelings and opinions arrive from the use of positive images to characterize one's group. For example, my group, whatever it might be, is hard-working, loyal, honest and good-looking. If you are not part of my group then you do not share these traits.

The Red Devils and the Bull Dogs: A summer camp adventure

Mufazer Sherif ran an experiment with 24 boys from relatively similar backgrounds, all protestant, 12-year olds (Sherif and Sherif, 1966). The boys were taken to a summer camp sponsored by the Yale Psychology Department for 18 days. None of the boys knew each other before camp. The first few days of the camp were devoted to identifying the preferences and inclinations of the boys before they were divided into groups. They were allowed to select who they sat near and slept near and all activities during those days were done as one large group. During these first few days the boys naturally clustered into groups of two or three. In the second stage of the experiment, these friendship clusters were split up as the boys were divided into two groups: the Red Devils and the Bull Dogs. Throughout the five days of the second stage of the experiment the boys participated in activities with their particular group. They were allowed to design insignia for their groups and make signs. Identification and loyalty developed among the members of both the Bull Dogs and the Red Devils. In the third stage of the experiment the two groups were brought together to participate in intentionally frustrating activities. A series of competitive games was played. Antagonism between the two groups developed and eventually erupted into fighting which led the experimenters to call off the remainder of the third stage of the experiment. Several days in the camping experiment remained and every attempt was made to dissolve the in-group out-group distinctions that had developed between the Red Devils and the Bull Dogs. However, the campers still made choices to sit down next to members of their in-group at meals and divisions between the two groups of boys persisted.

A campground is not a culture, nor is it a country. However, the experiment conducted by Sherif is both interesting and informative because it demonstrates the ease with which individuals form in-group and out-group definitions and the persistence of these ties. The experiment also demonstrated that stereotypes, once formed, do not easily disappear and tend to be very difficult to breakdown.

Feelings of cultural superiority in real life often have fairly important consequences as cultural superiority often legitimizes attempts at political control. An excellent example of this type of belief is the attitude of the Romans towards their subjects during the years of the Roman Empire. Roman citizens were given special rights in the territory controlled by the empire whereas other people, who lived within the borders of the empire but were not citizens, were not accorded the same set of rights. The Romans believed that they were superior to other groups that were under their control and established a system whereby those that were Roman received privileged status under the same government as others who did not. In spite of having a clearly unified government there were in-groups and out-groups within the Roman Empire.

OPPOSITIONAL GROUP FORMATION

Groups can emerge as a result of changing economic and political circumstances. It is also possible for groups to emerge because others define them collectively. In other words, they emerge through no specific action of their own. This typically occurs with groups that are either being blamed for some social ill (as in the case of the Tutsis in Rwanda) or are being defined as 'other' to legitimize or enable socioeconomic inequalities. We can refer to powerful ethnic or nationalized groups within a society as being in-groups.

Powerful in-groups can define lower status out-groups at their own discretion. This definition of out-groups has enormous potential to create conflict. Nationalism and the mobilization of ethnic groups rests on the past, but is articulated in present political and economic contexts and often defines itself in opposition to other groups within a community. We can think of this type of oppositional definition of ethnic identities in a negative or ambivalent context. It is negative when an in-group defines itself in opposition to an out-group in order to express superiority or gain some sort of advantage over the out-group. We can see examples of this sort of out-group definition almost anytime we see instances of slavery. Slavery in practice is so inhumane that there is typically an attempt to justify it or minimize the guilt of the perpetrators by reference to the enslaved group as somehow being less than human. This expression of superiority clearly defines in-group and out-group in a way that attempts to bring some justification to the practice.

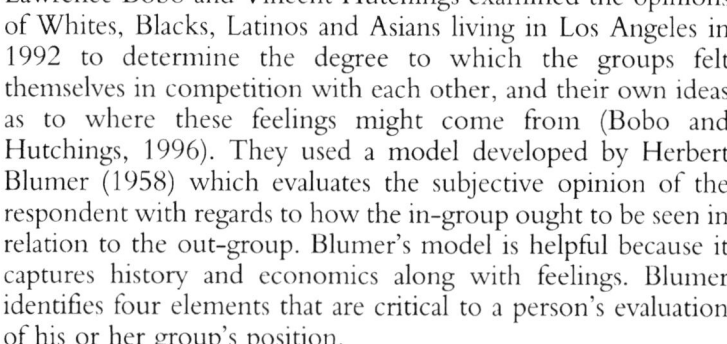

In and Out in LA

Lawrence Bobo and Vincent Hutchings examined the opinions of Whites, Blacks, Latinos and Asians living in Los Angeles in 1992 to determine the degree to which the groups felt themselves in competition with each other, and their own ideas as to where these feelings might come from (Bobo and Hutchings, 1996). They used a model developed by Herbert Blumer (1958) which evaluates the subjective opinion of the respondent with regards to how the in-group ought to be seen in relation to the out-group. Blumer's model is helpful because it captures history and economics along with feelings. Blumer identifies four elements that are critical to a person's evaluation of his or her group's position.

1 a belief about the superiority of the in-group

2 a belief in the difference in the out-group

3 a belief that the in-group is entitled to certain 'rights and privileges'

4 an understanding that those 'rights and privileges' are desired by the out-group

Bobo and Hutchings determined that among Blacks, Latinos, Asians and Whites there was a perception that the other groups were threats because of their competition for social resources. The reasons why each group perceived the others as threatening were different in each pair.

It is not necessarily the case that out-group definition would occur because of some sort of intended exploitation. Historically, we can identify some oppositional group formation that has appeared intentionally ambivalent. An excellent example of the importance of opposition to an out-group in the development of ethnic and national identities comes from Wales. Welsh identity developed in opposition to English identity. It was, during all but a few years of English history, not the intent of the English to exploit nor to explicitly dominate and control the Welsh.

When was Wales?

Gwyn Williams, a Welshman writing on Welsh identity, has argued that historically the Welsh are difficult to identify. Williams argues that the Welsh were, in the end, defined by the English (Williams, 1985). It could be argued that the English were originally Welsh, or at least the two were indistinguishable. The rise of the English empire and its strengthening through the eleventh century turned the land of Wales into a marginal area on the outskirts of a growing empire. Even the name 'Welsh' comes from the English. The original Welsh referred to themselves as Cymry. During the Tudor Century (1485–1603) Wales became Protestant, and in the eighteenth century Wales was the home of a Calvinist Methodist movement independent of the English Methodist movement. This religious revival, along with the industrial revolution, created a nascent Welsh nation in the nineteenth century. However, the Great Depression eliminated any serious manifestations of Welsh identity as many Welsh left Wales for greener pastures and better opportunities elsewhere. Williams argues that the Welsh have 'no historical autonomy'. They have survived through the ages through a miracle that has come from being British. 'Welsh identity has constantly renewed itself by anchoring itself in variant forms of Britishness' (Williams, 1982). Welsh identity has waxed and waned over time depending on economic and historical circumstances in England. When the English economy has been healthy, Welsh identity has waned. When the economy in England has declined, Welsh identity has become more popular. Thus Williams concludes that 'Wales is an artifact which the Welsh produce; the Welsh make and remake Wales day by day and year by year. If they want to' (Williams, 1982).

In the Welsh example above we have an occasion of out-group identity formed by opposition which is, for the most part, ambivalent. The English did not set about to define a group of people called the Welsh either by their explicit behaviour or by any type of social distancing. The Welsh case demonstrates several interesting issues. First, it is clear in the case of the Welsh that the issue of identity really is a choice. One can choose to learn Welsh, choose to give children Welsh names and choose to learn to sing in close harmony. Alternatively, one can choose to reject these behaviours and simply become English. It is, and some would argue it always has been, an option to be Welsh.

The second interesting issue that the Welsh case raises is the role of the government in providing institutions (like the Welsh assembly created after a 1997 referendum) that promote ethnic identities and even nationalist movements. The regionalization of ethnic groups or the official recognition of particular groups is likely to cause nationalism to take root even where it did not previously exist. Wales is not the only example. States that have used ethnic identities as a mechanism for dividing the country up into units, Yugoslavia and Ethiopia are examples, have created ethnic conflicts and exacerbated those that previously existed. Joane Nagel (Nagel, 1986) has argued that when a state officially recognizes ethnic groups there are two possible effects:

1 An increase in the level of ethnic mobilization among all ethnic groups and

2 A determination of the boundaries and the rules for competition between ethnic groups

An increase in ethnic mobilization is not necessarily positive, particularly if it leads to violence. However, the second effect, setting of the rules for competition between ethnic groups, can be beneficial. A state which is able to manage the competition of ethnic groups can potentially channel nationalist agendas that might become violent into democratic political practices. An example, of how a state might go about doing this can be found in the chapter on Northern Ireland (Chapter Seven).

COMPETITION THEORY

Competition theory argues that group political identities are defined and strengthened when groups in close proximity to one another have to struggle over the rights to scarce resources. The struggle over resources explains the origins and disappearance of ethnic groups as well as providing an explanation for why they appear to be politically more important at some times and not others. It is the goal of competition theory to try and explain the conditions under which ethnic identities become more important than other types of identity (Olzak and Nagel, 1986), as such it shows us how socially constructed identities come into being. Many scholars view competition theory as particularly helpful in explaining why ethnicity is of critical importance in developing countries. They argue that it is the stress of economic and political development, or what some might call modernization, that leads to ethnic movements. Chapter Eight, the case study of Eritrea, provides a case that readers can use to evaluate competition theory.

The struggle for resources within a society leads to the rise and decline of ethnic groups and can even give birth to new ethnic groups. Competition theorists would argue that this is as true for developed countries as it is for developing countries. An example of how the competition for resources can lead to a strengthening of ethnic identity or a mobilization of an ethnic group into a nationalist group is the case of Scotland.

The Scottish nationalist movement took off in Scotland after the discovery of oil just off the Scottish coast. The presence of such an important resource within their territory gave the Scots a reason to be Scottish again. Gaining control of the revenue from the oil and ensuring that it did not go exclusively to the British government was one of the focal points of the Scottish nationalist movement.

North Sea oil

In the mid-1970s, oil was discovered in the North Sea off the Scottish coast. Though the majority of the oil proceeds are handled by the government of the United Kingdom, the discovery of oil fuelled the Scottish economy, creating industry-related jobs. Though the economy of the United Kingdom as a whole took a slump in the mid-1970s and early 1980s, the Scottish national economy remained steady. This caused an increase in Scottish national sentiment, as many Scots began to believe that their economy could be strong enough to support an independent Scotland.

Robert Thomsen (Thomsen, 2001) argues that the oil discovery did not have quite the economic impact that was originally anticipated, so Scotland turned from economics to cultural nationalism to keep the fire burning. The rise in number of voters for the Scottish National Party over the past three decades is a definite indication that the Scottish nationalism that revived with the discovery of oil remains strong.

Competition theory provides some of the reasoning behind social constructivist arguments about ethnic identity formation. Ethnic identities form as groups organize to take advantage of some sort of resource opportunity. The role of leadership from this perspective is less important than it is in instrumentalist theories of political identity, but the idea of organizing to take advantage of certain opportunities is similar. In the case of the Scots we see that, once organized to take advantage of an economic opportunity, the group remained organized and has moved strategically over the past thirty years to redefine Scottish identity and make it more politically significant than it has been for hundreds of years.

CRITICISMS OF SOCIAL CONSTRUCTIVISM

Social constructivism has been criticized for being solely concerned with group formation rather than group goals and political agendas. This is an apt criticism. It is certainly the case that social constructivism can explain why a group is formed and why a group might disappear. Yet, what a group does in between formation and disappearance and how it achieves its goals is simply not a focus of the theory. This is the critical difference between the instrumentalist position and that of the social constructivists. Instrumentalists tend to be far more concerned with the goals of ethnic groups once they are formed. Because social constructivism is less focused on goals, the role of individuals in manipulating and constructing ethnic identities or nationalist agendas is not a major issue for social constructivists

The theory of social constructivism has also been criticized for not being sufficiently sensitive to the longevity of certain ethnic groups past the point when they seem to have any economic or political value. Some last far past the point of usefulness, and unlike the Germans in New York City, they do not seem to disappear. Why? Perhaps ethnic identities that do not carry negative associations, such as Latvian or Lithuanian, will be retained far longer. But when do they disappear? We do not really know and the social constructivist theory does not take us far enough in explaining the empirical causes of the disappearance of ethnic groups.

In the next section of the book, case studies of nationalist movements are presented. At the end of each chapter there is a section in which the theories of ethnicity and political identification are revisited. Some of these theories apply better to certain cases than to others. This is the frustrating nature of theoretical approaches to the real world – sometimes they fit and sometimes they don't. The strengths and weaknesses of each of these theories are illustrated in the way they can or cannot explain what is happening in the cases.

YOU DECIDE

What is the set of possible identities from which you can choose? Do you really believe that you have a choice to have one ethnic identity over another? Why or why not?

What might influence your choice of identities?

Do you have any experience of in-group and out-group formation? Was it based on ascribed traits such as height, skin colour, age or sex – or just the circumstances at the time?

Bibliography

Anderson, B. (1991) *Imagined Communities: Reflections on the Origin and Spread of Nationalism.* New York: Verso.

Bell, D. (1975) 'Ethnicity and Social Change', in *Ethnicity: theory and experience*, edited by N. Glazer and D. P. Moynihan. Cambridge, MA: Harvard University Press.

Blumer, H. (1958) 'Race Prejudice as a Sense of Group Position', *Pacific Sociological Review* 1:3–7.

Bobo, L., and Hutchings, V.L. (1996) 'Perceptions of Racial Group Competition', *American Sociological Review* 61 (6):951–72.

Connor, W. (1994) *Ethnonationalism.* Princeton, NJ: Princeton University Press.

Glazer, N., and Moynihan, D.P. (1963) *Beyond the Melting Pot.* Cambridge, MA: MIT and Harvard University Press.

Gourevitch, P. (1998) *We Wish to Inform You that Tomorrow We Will Be Killed with Our Families.* New York: Picador Press.

Harrison, D. (1981) *The White Tribe of Africa.* Berkeley, CA: University of California Press.

LeBaron, A. (1993) 'The Creation of the Modern Maya', in *The Rising Tide of Cultural Pluralism*, edited by C. Young. Madison, WI: University of Wisconsin Press.

Mair, L. (1974) *African Societies*. New York: Cambridge University Press.

Nagel, J. (1986) 'The Political Construction of Ethnicity', in *Competitive Ethnic Relations*, edited by J. Nagel. New York: Academic Press.

Olzak, S., and Nagel, J., eds. (1986) *Competitive Ethnic Relations*. New York: Academic Press, Inc.

Sherif, M., and Sherif, C.W. (1966) *Groups in Harmony and Tension*. New York: Octagon Books, Inc.

Thomsen, R. (2001) *Selves and Others of Political Nationalism in Stateless Nations: National Identity-Building Processes in the Modern Histories of Scotland and Newfoundland*, Copenhagen: Aarhus University.

Williams, G.A. (1985) *When was Wales?* London: Black Raven Press.

CHAPTER 5

Quebec

No single word exists, within Canada itself, to designate with satisfaction to both races a native of the country. When those of the French language use the word Canadien, they nearly always refer to themselves. They know their English-speaking compatriots as les Anglais. English-speaking citizens act on the same principle. They call themselves Canadians; those of the French language French Canadians.

[MacLennan 1945]

How is it that in the middle of English speaking North America, there is a French-speaking enclave that composes almost 25 per cent of the Canadian population? And how is it that this enclave has continued to exist rather than becoming integrated and ultimately assimilated into the English speaking territory of Canada? The answer begins with the history of colonization and the struggle between the British and the French for control of North America. The existence of French-speaking Quebec within an English-speaking Canada gives testimony to the history of the attempt of two European countries to draw North America into their sphere and ultimately into their control via the process of colonization.

	Total Population	English Speaking	French Speaking
Canada	28,528,125	16,890,615 59%	6,636,660 23%
Quebec	7,045,080	586,435 8%	5,700,150 81%

Statistics Canada. 'Population by Mother Tongue, 1996 Census.' http://www.statcan.ca/english/Pgdb/demo18a.htm, accessed November 2002.

As in many other parts of the world, it was trade and the attempt to exploit natural resources that preceded colonization. Both the English and the French attempted to establish control of the coastal areas of Canada near Newfoundland in order to capitalize on the fishing industry there. However, the interior areas of the country were not explored until Jacques Cartier, a French explorer and fur trader, discovered the St. Lawrence River. On July 24, 1534, Cartier put a thirty foot cross at the shore of the Gaspe Harbour that read 'Vive le

Roi de France'. This was the first French claim to North America. The French then proceeded to establish a colony in what was to become Quebec. However, due to the rugged nature of the land and the climate, the French were never able to consolidate control over the coastal fishing and fur trade of the area they referred to as 'New France'. They were in competition with the English and some of the Indian groups who were also trying to control the fur trade. The French were originally much less concerned with establishing settlements and colonies and focused their attention on controlling trade. The French formed an alliance with the Huron Indians and together they resisted attempts by the English–Iroquois alliance to take control of Quebec in 1628.

In 1670, the Hudson's Bay Trading Company was formed; and the English officially established control of parts of modern-day Canada. From that point on, there was open competition between the British and the French over the fur trade. This competition culminated in The Seven Year's War from 1756–1763. The English won, and the terms of the peace treaty ending the war forced the accession of most of the French territory east of the Mississippi River. The English control of Canada was thus firmly established.

The Conquest

The British conquest of Quebec took place in the middle of the Seven Years' War (1756–63) fought by Britain and France over trading rights in North America. The British, who had colonized all of what are now known as the original thirteen American colonies, had a greater number of people in the New World and were looking to expand their holdings. However, as the British colonists attempted to expand west and north beyond the Appalachian Mountains, they ran into the French trading territory of the Ohio Valley and the present-day province of Quebec; war ensued.

After spending the summer of 1759 encamped along the St. Lawrence River, outside of the city of Quebec, British Naval General James Wolfe saw his chance to capture the French-controlled city. The Marquis de Montcalm, the French officer in charge of Quebec, knew that if his city could survive under siege until the fall, the British would be forced to leave as they could not survive the winter on the river with no supplies. General Wolfe also knew this and, using his knowledge of the land surrounding Quebec, discovered a little-known path that enabled his army to scale the riverside cliffs and engage the surprised French troops on the Plains of Abraham. On these plains surrounding Quebec, the British defeated the French and pressed through to take the city. The province of Quebec was now a British possession.

The Seven Years' War was ended in 1763 by the Treaty of Paris, which formally ceded the French territory in Canada to the British Empire. In 1867, Quebec was formally incorporated as a province into the country of Canada.

In 1774, the English government passed the Quebec Act. This act recognized the French language in Quebec as well as French civil law for non-criminal matters, allowed Catholics to hold official positions, and allowed the Catholic Church to collect tithes from the population. The American colonies felt threatened by the provisions of the Quebec Act. They were uncomfortable with the role the church was given and the French Catholic nature of the province, given its close proximity to the colonies. Indeed, one of the first things that the American Continental Congress did in 1775 was to declare a trade embargo with Canada, in part due to the Quebec Act.

In 1837/8, Louis-Joseph Papineau led an armed revolt of French-speakers and others against British domination and authoritarian rule. The revolt, which was rather easily crushed, focused on the political and economic grievances of French Canadians who resented the demands of what was, at that point in time, an English speaking minority. At issue during the revolt was religion as well as economics. There was fear among French Canadians that, as Roman Catholics, they would be threatened by an overwhelmingly Protestant British Colonial Office. This fear was exacerbated by the Durham Report which was a British Colonial Office document published in 1838 encouraging the assimilation of French Canadians. In 1867, this concern was addressed in part by the establishment of a Canadian state by the British North America Act, which is the current basis of the Canadian Constitution.

FRANCOPHONE NATIONALISM

A sense of ethnic identity among the French-speaking people of Quebec has remained since the establishment of the Canadian state in 1867. There has always been a concern within the French Canadian community for the protection of its cultural identity and separate language. However, ethnicity was generally viewed as religious and cultural; the political element was not emphasized. After the Second World War a wave of historical revisionism occurred, the ultimate result of which was the development of a French Canadian political agenda. This amounted to a complete redefinition of French Canadian goals. Political goals now took precedence over religious and cultural issues.

The Quebec *nationalist* movement began in earnest in the early 1960s. Within the francophone population of Quebec there was a growing belief that national autonomy of some sort would protect the linguistic and cultural distinctiveness of the French-speaking community. Some French Canadians believed that the province of Quebec should not be viewed simply on equal terms with the other English speaking Canadian provinces, but must somehow have a special status or be completely separate due to the special needs of maintaining a threatened culture. Other French Canadians did view and still continue to view Quebec as a province like all the others.

'The revenge of the cradle' (revanche du burceau)

The so-called 'revenge of the cradle' refers to the high birth rates among the francophone Quebecers – birth rates that prevented the Anglophones from dominating the population of Quebec even after they took power. In the eighteenth and nineteenth centuries, the birthrate among French Canadians was very high. Until the 1960s, when the Liberal Party came into power, Quebec's society was dominated by the Catholic Church, which prohibits the use of contraceptives. This contributed to the high birth rates among the population.

In the 1960s, with the onset of the Quiet Revolution (see below) and the general liberalization of culture, many French Catholic Quebecers turned away from the church, claiming that it kept them poor and backward. They began using contraceptives; and women, who were previously tied to the home due to their many childcare duties, began entering the workforce. The general expansion of education among women exacerbated this trend. As a result, birth rates among French Canadians dropped dramatically and continued to decline. In 1996 there were 85,000 births among French Canadians, just four years later the birthrate had declined to 75,800 (Schuster 2001). Since the 'revenge of the cradle' ended in the 1970s, the French Canadians have gone from having one of the highest birth rates in the Western hemisphere to having one of the lowest.

In 1988, the Liberal government, which, ironically, had brought about the downfall of the 'revenge of the cradle' in the first place, began paying French Canadians to have children. A woman would be paid $500 for the first child she bore, $1000 for the second, and $8000 for the third. This policy was ended in 1997 by the Parti Québécois (PQ), the separatist party ruling Quebec at that time. The PQ instituted a programme of a $5 per

---

day subsidy for parents placing their children in daycare, which was not as popular as the Liberal Party program, as evidenced by yet another drop in birth rates (Schuster, 2001).

THE QUIET REVOLUTION

The Quiet Revolution was ushered in with the election of Jean Lesage and the Liberal party to the government of Quebec in 1958. However, its intellectual foundations began much earlier. During the 1940s and 1950s French Canadian nationalism was predominantly rural and Catholic. There were no clear aspirations for a separate state. Politics in Quebec during the 1940s and 1950s were controlled by the Union Nationale party. The Union Nationale was corrupt, relying on vote buying and coercion to win elections. However, the party was viewed by many French Canadians as the defender of the Catholic Church in Quebec, so there was a mixing of nationalism and religion in the foundations of support for the Union Nationale.

In the late 1950s, Pierre Trudeau and a cohort of new French Canadian intellectuals appeared on the political scene as writers for a small literary magazine called *Cité libre*. The Cité libre group, as they were called, argued that the fundamental problem with Quebec was a lack of democracy. They developed a critical approach to the French Canadian nationalism of the past, which they viewed as being far too religiously driven and traditional. They were critical of the call for any institutional changes approaching independence, arguing that Quebec had plenty of power; it had simply not used it effectively to achieve francophone objectives within Canada. Trudeau formed his own party to fight for democratic reform in Quebec, but it never achieved electoral success. By 1960, the Quebec nationalist movement, including the Cité libre group, had united with the Liberal Party under the leadership of Jean Lesage and the Quiet Revolution began.

During the 1960s, with Lesage at the helm, Quebec began to focus on its economic development, modernization and the control of the apparatus of the state within the province. There was a specific attempt to address the issue of the ethnic division of labour, as most of the working class in Quebec was francophone, while the elites and business managers tended to be Anglophone. Ramsey Cook has identified the impact that this had on the francophone Quebecers. 'An economy where corporate managers operated in English was an economy where French Canadians rarely became corporate managers' (Cook, 1995: 133). Thus, the Quiet Revolution was set apart from prior ethnic movements because of its explicitly political goals.

Jean Lesage

Born in 1912 in Montreal, Jean Lesage was a lawyer who entered politics in 1945. He held a seat in the Quebec House of Commons from 1945 until 1958, when he was elected leader of the Liberal Party of Quebec. The Liberals were nationalist, though not separatist. They maintained that Quebec could preserve its distinct culture and traditions by remaining within the Canadian federal system as long as they were granted increasing autonomy. Several other nationalist leaders developed under the leadership of Lesage in the 1960s Quebec parliament including René Lévesque, Pierre Laporte and Jean Chretien. Jean Lesage retired from political life in 1970, and died quietly in 1980.

The Quiet Revolution had several effects noted below:

1 The state replaced the church as the dominant institution in the lives of French Canadians, including supplanting the church in the areas of education and health.

2 Quebec established its own Ministry of Education and attained provincial control over economic development efforts.

3 French Canadians began identifying themselves differently. They began to less frequently refer to themselves as French Canadians, and increasingly as Québécois.

4 They developed a political agenda 'une province pas comme les autres' or 'A province unlike the others'.

5 Language replaced religion as the critical nationalist issue.

In the 1960s the Quiet Revolution was transformed as the nationalist movement became very noisy indeed. Quebec nationalist groups began to push their agenda politically as they had never done before. Freed by socioeconomic growth within Quebec and a movement of the population from the rural areas to the urban centers, nationalist voices became loud and occasionally violent.

A Quebec separatist group, the Quebec Liberation Front (FLQ) was formed in the 1960s with a socialist agenda and the willingness to do whatever it took to bring about the secession of Quebec. Their terrorist activities began with mailbox bombings in the mid-1960s, but soon progressed to a more extreme terrorism. In 1970, the FLQ instigated what came to be known as the October Crisis, kidnapping two people and killing one of them. On October 5, 1970, FLQ members kidnapped British Trade Commissioner Jasper Cross, who was in Canada on government business. Five days later, on October 10, Canadian Labour Minister Pierre Laporte was kidnapped from his home near Montreal. He was killed one week later. In exchange for the return of Cross, the FLQ kidnappers demanded the release – and safe passage to Cuba – of 23 of their members who were political prisoners in Canada, as well as the front page publication of the FLQ manifesto in every major newsletter. After Laporte's murder, the Canadian government gave into the first demand, and Cross was freed early in December. The October Crisis, however, led Premier Bourassa to request that then Prime Minister Pierre Trudeau invoke the War Measures Act for six months, which allowed for searches, arrests, and detentions of citizens without a warrant. The FLQ has not had a major impact on Canadian politics since that time. The only other period in which the political conflict of the French Canadians turned violent occurred in October of 2000, when a spate of attacks occurred against 'The Second Cup' coffee shops. The attacks were carried out by the Brigade d'Autodéfense du Français (BAF), which objected to a government ruling that The Second Cup shops could keep their English names in Quebec.

One of the unique features of Quebec nationalism is the fact that it has generally been peaceful and democratic rather than violent. In fact, as the FLQ became violent in October of 1970 their popularity declined, illustrating the distaste for political violence in the pursuit of French Canadian goals. The Canadian government has always shown a great deal of flexibility and accommodation toward the francophone population. The comparative peacefulness of the nationalist movement among French-speaking Canadians has almost certainly been a result of the fact that the Canadian government has always allowed them a political voice and responded in an accommodating and flexible manner.

René Lévesque formed the Parti Québécois (PQ) in 1968 after leaving the Liberal Party. The PQ did not do well in elections at first, but by 1976 they had gained control of the provincial parliament and called for a referendum on independence for Quebec. The PQ supported a policy of sovereignty-association with regard to Canada. Sovereignty-association referred to an arrangement whereby Quebec would have political autonomy, but an ongoing economic partnership with Canada, sharing the same currency and the same economic policy. However, in 1968, the same year that Lévesque left the Liberal Party, Pierre Trudeau became prime minister of Canada.

In the 1970s, the Quebec nationalist movement was divided by a dispute that raged between two vocal and opposed French Canadians: Pierre Trudeau and René Lévesque. Trudeau advocated a Quebec nationalism fully expressed within the state of Canada. He thought the best interests of Quebec would always be served by a strong link to the Canadian economy. It is odd that Trudeau, who was one of Canada's

René Lévesque

René Lévesque was the original founder of the Parti Québécois (PQ), the political party that advocated a position of sovereignty-association with Canada. Before becoming a politician, Lévesque was a television news anchor. Lévesque served the Quebec Parliament as a member of the Liberal Party from 1960–1966, as a member of the cabinet of Jean Lesage. In 1967, Lévesque left both office and party in order to found the Parti Québécois. After several failed attempts to win office, he came to power as prime minister of Quebec in 1976, an office which he continued to hold until 1985. In 1987, Lévesque died of a heart attack. He is still remembered today as the figurehead of Quebec nationalism and the sovereignist movement.

strongest historical advocates of French representation within a federal state, should himself be a French speaker from Quebec. This fact suggests the complexity of the identity issues in this particular case. Some of the explanation lies in the fact that Trudeau was bilingual and thought that everyone else should be. Lévesque was also a French Canadian, but his support for sovereignty-association in Quebec came from an understanding of his own identity that excluded identification with a bilingual Canada. Lévesque said that he was a Quebecer first, a French-speaking Canadian second, and he had no other nationalist sentiment. He did not feel Canadian in any way (Cook, 1995: 140). Lévesque campaigned through his party for a referendum on the sovereignty-association of Quebec.

Pierre Trudeau

Pierre Elliot Trudeau was born on October 18, 1919, in Quebec to a wealthy French Canadian lawyer and his Scottish wife. Though he was from Quebec, Trudeau was against the secession of Quebec from Canada.

Trudeau's political career began in the 1950s when he began working with labour unions in Quebec while teaching constitutional law at his *alma mater*, the University of Montreal. It was also during this time that he founded and wrote extensively for his political journal, *Cité libre*. Trudeau always supported the point of view that the best interests of Quebec could be achieved in a united Canada. In 1965, he ran for the Canadian Parliament as a member of the Liberal Party. He won the seat and the position of Minister of Justice as well.

In 1968, Trudeau became leader of Canada's Liberal Party. Soon thereafter, he became prime minister. He was incredibly popular with Canadians of every demographic – in fact, he was so popular that the term 'Trudeaumania' was coined in Canada. Trudeau's fascinating personal life was partly the cause of his overwhelming popularity. In 1971, at the age of fifty-two, he married Margaret Sinclair, a twenty-two year old woman that he had met while vacationing in Tahiti. He and Margaret had three children before they were divorced in 1977. In 1992, Trudeau fathered a child out of wedlock by a constitutional law expert, Deborah Coyne. Several years later, in 1998, his youngest son was tragically killed in an avalanche. Trudeau's personality naturally endeared him to the public; he was a charismatic leader, he dressed stylishly and he drove sports cars. He was perhaps the most popular Canadian Prime Minister of the twentieth century.

In all, Trudeau spent sixteen years as prime minister of Canada, serving from 1968–1979 and 1980–1984. After his retirement from politics, he practiced law in Montreal until he died on September 28, 2000.

In 1980, Lévesque won his battle for a referendum on political sovereignty for Quebec. But Trudeau won the day, partly because he promised that a 'no' vote was not a vote for the status quo. Independence for Quebec was defeated by a vote of 41.8 per cent to 58.2 per cent. But what then? The situation with Quebec was not resolved; its place in Canada was not fully determined and there were several ongoing jurisdictional battles between the government of Canada and the provincial government of Quebec. In 1982 the situation only got worse as Canada patriated its constitution so that it could make amendments. The Constitution of Canada was composed of the British North America Act of 1867 (now renamed the Constitution Act), other constitution acts, a Charter of Rights and Freedoms, similar to the Bill of Rights, and other provisions. The 1982 constitution gave all 10 provinces an equal voice in the federal government and added the Charter of Rights and Freedoms to the constitution, which protected French as one of the two national languages as well as assuring basic civil liberties. The legislature of Quebec, fearing that their province's language and culture were at risk, rejected the constitution, putting Quebec in an ambiguous legal situation. The province was within Canada, yet it had not ratified the constitution of Canada, in spite of the fact that it was governed by that constitution. Despite some efforts at compromise to get Quebec to ratify the constitution, there was little advancement under the Trudeau governments. Trudeau was followed by Brian Mulroney, whose Conservative government, together with the premier of Quebec, Robert Bourassa and the premiers of the other Canadian provinces, negotiated the Meech Lake Accord of 1987.

At Meech Lake it was agreed that Quebec would be recognized as a 'distinct society' within Canada. However, this phrase turned out to be quite controversial, and the Meech Lake Accord failed because Newfoundland and Manitoba would not ratify it, believing, among other things, that the 'distinct society' wording elevated Quebec's status above the other provinces in the Canadian Federation. In English-speaking Canada the federation is viewed to be a federation of equal provinces. In Quebec, on the other hand, the federation is viewed by some to be between two people groups: the anglophones and the francophones. At Meech Lake there was no resolution to the disagreement. Thus, Meech Lake ended and Quebec had still not signed onto the Constitution Act of 1982. Its political status remained unclear. Mulroney tried again with the Charlottetown Agreement in 1992, an accord targeted at addressing not only the concerns of Quebec but also of indigenous people groups within Canada. The Charlottetown Agreement had the support of all the premiers of the ten provinces and also of some indigenous peoples groups, but it failed in a country-wide referendum. Since Charlottetown there has been little movement on this constitutional issue within Canada, and the position of Quebec within Canada remains uncertain.

The failure of Meech Lake led many French Canadians who had become members of the Canadian parliament under the Conservative and Liberal party banners to desert these parties and form the Bloc Québécois (BQ) under the leadership of Lucien Bouchard. In 1993, when the Conservative government ended, the BQ became the official government opposition party of the Canadian Parliament.

Lucien Bouchard

Lucien Bouchard was born in Quebec on December 22, 1938. He received his law degree at the University of Laval in 1964 and practiced privately until 1985, when he was appointed Canadian Ambassador to France. In 1998, Canadian Prime Minister Brian Mulroney appointed him Secretary of State. In the same year, he was elected a federal Member of Parliament from the Conservative party. He left that party in 1990 and, together with the other Quebec members of Parliament, formed the Bloc Québécois, a federal party committed to the autonomy of Quebec. Bouchard was both founder and leader of the BQ. He also became the prime minister of Quebec.

In 1993 the Parti Québécois (PQ) captured 54 out of the 75 seats in Quebec's parliament. The PQ again pushed for a referendum on independence, which occurred in 1995. The question on the ballot was negotiated by Quebec nationalists of a variety of political persuasions and that is apparent in the wording, which was:

> Do you agree that Quebec should become sovereign, after having made a formal offer to Canada for a new economic and political partnership, within the scope of the Bill Respecting the Future of Quebec, and of the agreement signed on June 12, 1995? (Keating, 2001: 95)

With an astonishing voter turnout of 93 per cent, the referendum was defeated, with an estimated 90 per cent of those Quebecers who were not francophone voting against it and only 60 per cent of francophone Quebecers voting in favour (Keating, 2001: 85). Following the referendum Bouchard resigned as a Member of the House of Commons. He took a seat in the Quebec Parliament, where he became prime minister of the province, as the PQ had a majority of seats. In 2001, Bouchard resigned his post as prime minister because he had not accomplished his goals, and felt that his usefulness in that office was over. Today, the situation remains unresolved. Support for sovereignty and autonomy consistently runs at about 30 per cent of the population of Quebec (Keating, 2001: 99).

Indigenous people

The issue of indigenous people presents itself in a variety of federal issues within the Canadian context. With several different groups making claims, a federal system of asymmetrical autonomy has developed over time. Indigenous groups have exerted power in a number of ways. Some, such as the Inuits in Nunavut, have become highly politically mobilized to the point where they were granted autonomy. Others use their power essentially as a veto, in the case of the Indians in Quebec. Overall, the Canadian government allows for autonomy to be decided on a case-by-case basis through negotiation with the central government as there is no norm within the constitution or other government document.

The ideas of autonomy developed in Quebec have been accompanied by calls for greater autonomy among the indigenous people of Canada. The Inuit have been the most vocal and also the most successful of the indigenous groups. With 26,000 residents living in an area that covers almost 20 per cent of the country's landmass, the Inuit make up 80 per cent of the population of the land where they live (Watts, 2000: 38). This concentration of population has enabled them to mobilize as a group as a means of being a political force in Canada. A 1999 referendum created the autonomous self-governing system of Nunavut.

A second indigenous group which has exerted political power are the Cree people in northern Quebec. With 95 per cent voting against the separation of Quebec in the 1995 referendum, the Cree minority has expressed their fear of being a minority within a federal minority (Watts, 2000: 38). Claiming the right to separate from Quebec if Quebec has the right to separate from Canada, the Cree have been a motivating factor in Quebec's continuing link to the Canadian central government. Furthermore, the vast amount of resources available in the region the Cree live creates incentive for Quebec to work with them through the federal process, desiring to attain their vote in the issue of sovereignty while keeping them a part of any form of autonomous Quebec.

LANGUAGE

In Canada, the issue of language is fascinating because it has taken on such clearly economic as well as cultural overtones. Prior to the Quiet Revolution it was argued by many on both sides of the nationalism debate that a country should have a single language. Thus, the French-speakers had justification for a desire for independence and the English-speakers had justification for their push for assimilation. Also important were the issues of language in education and what types of schools would be funded by the government. However, during the Quiet Revolution the argument regarding language became further politicized by the addition of economic studies showing that French speaking Canadians tended to be on the lower rungs of the economic ladder (Cook, 152). As the Canadian state grew in the years after the Second World War, the issue of civil service positions and language requirements for state employment became important. French-speaking Canadians wanted to be able to work for the state and to receive state services in their own language. Thus, the pressure for a clear definition of the language position of the state became more intense as the bureaucracy grew.

Within Quebec, the language issue is even more politically complex. Although the majority of people within Quebec speak French as their native language, it is not the only language spoken. The Ungava region, which was incorporated into Quebec by the Canadian national government in 1912, composes a large part of the territory of Quebec. This region consists of a majority of native peoples who speak neither French nor English as their first language. If Quebec couches its nationalist aspirations in terms of language, what of the people living in Ungava? Should they too be able to secede? Moreover, what of the largely English speaking West End of Montreal? Will they be forced to speak French only? The problems that exist in creating a linguistic nationalism have led the nationalist movement in Quebec to focus their aspirations on territory and a kind of civic nationalism rather than an ethnic nationalism. An ethnic nationalism based on language excludes 11 per cent of the population of Quebec; that said, language remains an important political issue.

Legislation in Canada regarding language is also complex. Few laws specifically addressed language until Pierre Trudeau became prime minister in 1968. Trudeau was instrumental in developing the Official Languages Act, which gave equality to French within the public service. However, since all provinces have the right to control language and education within their territories, Quebec also passed a language law called Bill 101. It was passed in 1976, after the PQ came to power in the province. Bill 101 made French the *only* official language in Quebec. It made French the language of both education and economics in the province. Large companies were forced to conduct their internal correspondence in French, and French education was compulsory for everyone except the anglophone population in Quebec. This specifically meant that immigrants coming to Quebec who spoke neither French nor English must be educated in French. The Canadian government may have been willing to compromise on the issue of language, but the provincial government would not.

Bill 101

Bill 101 requires that business advertising in Quebec be in French; if there is English present on the sign, the French words must be at least twice as large. The implementation of Bill 101 was facilitated by 1974's Bill 22, which established French as the only official language of Quebec. The Official Languages Act, which was passed by the Canadian Parliament in 1969, was another precursor, as it stated that both English and French were official languages of Canada and all government activities would transpire in both.

Though Bill 101 was seen as a victory for the majority francophone population in Quebec, it aggravated the anglophones, who had dominated the province's business community. In 1988, a case came before the Canadian Supreme Court that embodied the anglophones' frustration with Bill 101. This case, formally known as *Quebec (Attorney General) v. La Chaussure Brown's Inc. et Al.*, was brought forth by the province of Quebec, which penalized an anglophone business owner for naming his shoe store in English. The defendant claimed that the right to conduct business in the language of one's choice was a fundamental right guaranteed by the Quebec Charter and the Canadian Charter. The court agreed, ruling that the language legislation was unconstitutional under both charters, stating, in effect, that too high a percentage of Quebec's population spoke English to justify the exclusivity of French for practical purposes.

The ruling in the Brown Shoes case paved the way for yet another piece of legislation dealing with language: Bill 178. Passed a few days after the Supreme Court decision in 1988, Bill 178 retained all of the provisions of Bill 101, except that it allowed businesses to advertise in English *inside* their stores, as long as they also advertised in French.

Currently, Quebecers whose mother tongue is French make up 82 per cent of the province. Only 8 per cent of all residents speak no French. Moreover, 88 per cent of persons born in Quebec stay in Quebec, rather than moving elsewhere in Canada or out of the country (Lemco, 1994: 18).

THE INTERNATIONAL DIMENSION

One of the major issues that would need to be addressed if Quebec is successful at achieving full sovereignty is that of treaties and relationships with other states. Article 9 of the Bill on Quebec's Sovereignty, written in 1995, states that Quebec would accede to all treaties of which Canada is a part. Another question remains: would other states recognize, or even support, an independent Quebec?

Two states, the United States and France, are of special importance to Quebec. The United States, as Canada's primary trading partner, wants to be sure that the dispute between Quebec and the rest of Canada does not lead to upheaval that would disrupt the tenor of their trading relationship. Thus, the US stance on Quebec secessionism is determined not by a preference for either side but rather by the desire for economic stability. The United States has held a steady position of non-interference. Former President George H.W. Bush called for the United States to 'courageously sit on the sidelines' in the Quebec dispute (Parizeau, 1995: 71). It has been the US position that any discussion of the recognition of Quebec by the US government would come only after Quebec and the rest of Canada had come to a deal on secession. Current US policy is the same and we can expect it to remain steady in the future.

The French hold a similar, though not identical policy, to the United States. Summing up their position as 'non-interference but not indifference' the French policy is explicitly ambiguous. During a 1996 visit, French Prime Minister Alain Juppé made a number of statements about standing by the side of Quebec while at the same time voicing a desire to be neutral and advocating a policy of non-intervention. The questionable comments gave rise to positive interpretations from both French Canadians and the Canadian government, as well as anger from others on both sides who thought his statements were not strong enough.

Thus, neither the French nor the United States are encouraging of the Quebec independence movement. Both countries tried to leave the politics to the Canadians. While this is not surprising in the case of the United States, which, because of its shared border and extensive trade, had an interest in maintaining good relationships with both sides in the conflict. It is more surprising in the French case, because the French have so often thrown their political support behind countries simply because they speak French. The lack of international support for the independence movement in Quebec can provide one potential explanation as to why the independence movement has lost steam in recent years. Perhaps the post-secession economic situation simply did not appear very appealing.

APPLYING THE THEORIES

How do we best understand the nationalism of the French Canadians? Why is it that a people who used to consider themselves simply culturally and religiously different from other Canadians are now advocating nearly complete independence? Perhaps revisiting our three bodies of theory can help answer these questions.

Primordialism

Perhaps the most frequently referenced primordialist scholar writing about Quebec is Jean Laponce (1985). Laponce argues that most people are unilingual. This is the way human beings are made; we prefer to use a single language. He has suggested that the rise of nationalism in Quebec is simply a result of increased contact between anglophone and francophone Canadians in the 1960s. The inborn resistance to bilingualism, coupled with the increased contact has led to political conflict. Though he may seem somewhat extreme, Laponce is not alone. Many scholars believe language to be the defining characteristic of ethnicity (Edwards, 1991: 269). This is because languages are not easily learned. As languages are more easily acquired in youth, unless a person learns another language quite early in life he or she will most likely speak it with some sort of accent. Therefore, language provides a clear identifier between in-groups and out-groups; it is a well-defined boundary of ethnic identification.

Instrumentalism

In the case of Quebec, it is clear that elites have used linguistic differences to further their own political agendas. Who benefits from policies such as Bill 101 that force companies to use French for their internal memos, meetings and correspondence? Clearly the franco-phone Canadians. Bill 101 elevates those who are bilingual in French and English above those who can speak only one language or the other. This ensures a place for the francophone elite and defines the nationalist struggle as a linguistic, rather than a cultural or religious struggle. Interestingly, in the case of Quebec the elites clearly chose not to emphasize religion or culture in defining the distinctiveness of their society. By the time the Quiet Revolution of the 1960s was over, language had become the focal point of conflict.

Social Constructivism

Prior to the Quiet Revolution in Quebec, there was a cultural division of labour with the French-speaking population occupying the lowest rungs of the socioeconomic system. French speakers were predominantly labourers, furriers, woodsmen and members of the working class. There was little room for them in the higher echelons of corporations within Canada, due to the fact that English was the sole language of communication in most companies. Given that this was the case, social constructivists can explain the development of nationalist sentiment in Quebec in the 1960s. They have a bit more trouble explaining why it hasn't gone away, particularly in light of legal remedies like Bill 101, which appear to eliminate the unequal playing field for French speakers in Quebec.

YOU DECIDE

Which theoretical approach do you find the most convincing?
Do linguistic differences necessarily lead to nationalism?
Do you think that we will see a decline in nationalism in Quebec in the future?
What might the impact of the experience of Quebec be on other groups within Canada such as native populations?

TIMELINE

1608   Territory of New France colonized by people of French origin, led by Samuel de Champlain.

1754–   Anglo-French War in North America (known as the
1763   French and Indian War to Americans), in which the British and French fought over territorial expansion and trading rights in the 'new world'.

1760   Britain claimed the city of Quebec for its own, following their defeat of France in 1759 at the Battle of Quebec (referred to by French Canadians as 'The Conquest', while allowing the people of Quebec to keep their language and religion. 'Revenge of the cradle' begins in Quebec.

1763   First Treaty of Paris ended the Anglo-French war and ceded Canada to Britain.

1774   Quebec Act: Britain formally took control over all of Quebec, reinstating the borders as they had been under the French; the British made provisions for religious freedom in Quebec.

1791   Constitution Act of 1791: granted Quebec its own parliament and separated it from the rest of Canada in title. 'Upper Canada': present-day Ontario, 'Lower Canada': Quebec. These actions gave Quebec limited autonomy until 1840.

1837–   Louis-Joseph Papineau leads French-speaking Canadians and
1838   upper Canada in armed revolt against their British rulers. The rebellion was crushed. Durham Report advocates assimilation.

1840   'Lower Canada' (Quebec) was forced to enter a united Canadian government and its separate parliament was taken away.

1867   British North America Act: created a federal system of government in Canada, reinstating parliaments in each province, including Quebec (partially in an attempt to make up for 1840).

1960   The Quebec Liberal Party, under Jean Lesage, won control of Quebec in parliamentary elections. Lesage became prime minister of Quebec from 1960–1966. Birth of the RIN (Rassemblement pour l'independence nationale). Beginning of the 'Quiet Revolution'.

1970   Parti Québécois won 24 per cent of the popular vote in Quebec. Led by René Lévesque, this nationalist party demanded separation and independence for Quebec.

1976   Parti Québécois comes to power in Quebec.

1980   First referendum vote on secession taken in Quebec. Secession was defeated by a vote of 41.8 per cent to 58.2 per cent.

1982 Constitution Act of 1982, by which Canada patriated its constitution from Britain. Quebec was the only province not to accept Canada's proposed new constitution.

1990 The Bloc Québécois, a party explicitly seeking independence, was formed, led by Lucien Bouchard.

1995 Second referendum vote on secession taken in Quebec. Again, secession was defeated, this time by a closer vote of 49.4 per cent to 51.6 per cent.

1998 Canada's Supreme Court ruled that if a 'clear majority' of people in Quebec wanted to secede, then Canada must allow it. However, Quebec cannot secede without the assent of the government of Canada.

USEFUL WEBSITES

http://www.premier.gouv.qc.ca/premier_ministre This is the official site of the prime minister of Quebec. It provides an overview of the major political events in Quebec's history.

http://www.facts.com/cd/v00076.htm Provides a synopsis of the two secession referendum votes in Quebec.

http://www.digitalhistory.org/qmap.html A map and detailed description of the 1759 British conquest of Quebec.

http://www.canadianembassy.org/government/quebec-e.asp A description of the history and role of Quebec within the Canadian federation from the position of the Canadian government.

http://law.about.com/library/weekly/aa082498.htm A description of the decision of the Supreme Court of Canada in the secession case, 1998

Bibliography

Anderson, F. (2000) *Crucible of War: The Seven Years' War and the Fate of Empire in British North America*, 1754–1766. New York: Alfred A. Knopf.

Barreto, A.A. (1998) *Language, Elites, and the State*, Westport, CT: Praeger

Cook, R. (1995) *Canada, Québéc and the Uses of Nationalism*. Second edn. Toronto: McClelland & Stewart Inc.

Keating, M. (2001) *Nations against the State*. Second edn. New York: Palgrave.

Laponce, J.A. (1985) 'Protecting the French Language in Canada', *Journal of Commonwealth and Comparative Politics* 23:157–70.

Lemco, J. (1994) *Turmoil in the Peaceable Kingdom*. Buffalo, NY: University of Toronto Press.

MacLennan, H. (1945) *Two Solitudes*. Toronto: Collins.

Parizeau, J. (1995) 'The Case for a Sovereign Quebec', *Foreign Policy* 99:69–77.

Watts, R.L. (2000) 'Federalism and Diversity in Canada', in *Ethnicity and Autonomy*, edited by Y. Ghai. New York: Cambridge University Press.

CHAPTER 6

Bosnia-Herzegovina

*When any community is subordinately connected with another, the great
danger of the connection is the extreme pride and self-complacency of the
superior, which in all matters of controversy will probably decide in its own
favour.*

[Edmund Burke 1975]

When most people think of Bosnia they recall a complicated conflict
that was notable in the media for the introduction of the term 'ethnic
cleansing'. The Bosnian War, and the disintegration of the former
Yugoslavia, was a painful object lesson in the politics of identity. It is
useful as a case study in this book as it illustrates the role of leadership
in articulating ethnic causes and leading people to identify with a
particular ethnic group, the example of shifting ethnic identities over
time and the clear refutation of the belief that violent ethnic conflict is
a problem of the developing world.

THE HISTORY OF IDENTITY

Critical to any analysis of the conflict in Bosnia is understanding how
there came to be three different ethnic groups in Bosnia and how they
define the boundaries of their ethnicity. Since the 1970s there have
been Serbs, Croats and Muslims all living in Bosnia. However, it was
not always the case that the Muslims defined themselves as an ethnic
group. In the past they have seen themselves as Muslim Serbs,
capturing two identities: one ethnic and one religious. It is only in the
past 30 years or so that they have emerged as a distinctly defined *ethnic*,
rather than religious, group.

Islam first came to Bosnia with the arrival of the Turk-controlled
Ottoman Empire in the fifteenth century. While the Turks occupied
all of Yugoslavia it was the Bosnian Serbs in particular who seemed
most attracted to Islam and who converted in large numbers. By the
early seventeenth century, Muslims became an absolute majority in
 Bosnia (Malcolm, 1994). Those that became Muslims were Bosnian
Serbs who had previously been Eastern Orthodox Christians.

Because of its strategic location in Europe, Bosnia has historically
been a focal point for conflict. In 1878 the Austro-Hungarian Empire

wrestled control of Bosnia away from the Ottoman Empire; as a result, many Muslims left Bosnia for Ottoman controlled areas. Exactly how many Muslims left at that time and in the years following is not known, estimates range between 60,000 and an improbably high 300,000 (Malcolm, 1994: 170).

The control of the Austro-Hungarian Empire did not continue past the First World War. In 1918 the empire collapsed, allowing for the formation of the first national government of Bosnia and Herzegovina. In 1920, elections were held for a constituent assembly that would write the constitution for the new Yugoslavian state of which Bosnia would be a part. However, there was disagreement as to how the state would be controlled. Serbs wanted a centralized Yugoslav state and the Croats sought some sort of decentralization in a regional arrangement. Serbs won the battle when a unitary state was formed. During this period Muslims began identifying themselves as Muslim Serbs and Muslims Croats, depending on which policy position they supported. Once the state of Yugoslavia was established there was an attempt to address the Croatian concerns for decentralization. Yugoslavia implemented a regionalization plan which gave some powers and responsibilities to sub-state regions just before the Second World War.

During the Second World War, Germany and Italy invaded and divided Yugoslavia. Communist resistance to the Axis occupation was led by Josip Broz Tito, who was half Croat and half Slovene. Tito was loyal to Stalin during the war and had two goals, to get rid of the Axis occupation and to launch a communist revolution. The communist forces were able to combine these two goals with great effectiveness.

Josip Broz Tito

Tito, born Josip Broz to a peasant family in Yugoslavia, was the son of a Croatian father and a Slovene mother. A poor peasant who reached the peak of political power, Tito single-handedly shaped the politics of Yugoslavia in the mid-twentieth century. A veteran of the First World War and an early supporter of the revolutionary Communists, Tito gained international recognition for his role in the Second World War. When the Axis powers invaded Yugoslavia, he raised bands of communist guerillas that effectively fought the Germans, the Italians, and Yugoslavia's royal ruling family. After the war, the Communist Party of Yugoslavia (CPY), of which he was secretary-general, emerged as the ruling party of Yugoslavia. Tito became president, an office which he maintained until his death in 1980 from cancer.

Though Tito's government was communist, relations with the Soviet Union were often strained by Tito's reluctance to

---

follow the demands of the Kremlin. In 1948, Stalin denounced Tito and tried to force his cooperation through economic pressure and increased border patrols. Pressure from the Soviets united Yugoslavians under Tito. Indeed, during the 35 years of his presidency, ethnic tension was hardly present. Many think that Tito's particular brand of socialism triumphed over ethnic differences in Yugoslavia. As if to prove this point, ethnic tensions within the former Yugoslavia escalated dramatically after his death.

Tito personally crafted a united Yugoslavia after the Second World War. However, he did not do so through persuasion alone, he also used violence against those who did not support his unification agenda. Although Tito's tenure as president of Yugoslavia provided an essential time of political stability and economic growth, his methods of maintaining control were not above reproach. It is widely known that Tito oppressed dissidents and sent them to work camps, much in the way that Stalin did. In the immediate aftermath of the Second World War, religious expression of any sort was repressed in keeping with communist ideology until 1954, when a law was passed guaranteeing religious freedom.

BECOMING ETHNICALLY MUSLIM

The establishment of 'Muslim' as an ethnic or political identity, rather than a religious identity, was led by communists and other secularized Muslims. Their distinct national identity is based on what Wieland (2001) refers to as the Bogomil myth – the idea that the Bosnian Muslims are descended from the medieval Bosnian aristocracy who converted to Islam after the Ottoman conquest in 1463, becoming the pillar of Ottoman rule in the Balkans. Wieland notes that this is most certainly untrue because people of all faiths converted to Islam; however, it is whether people believe the myth, rather than the truth of the myth that is most important, and this myth is widely believed.

Ethnic Muslim Yugoslavs were unable to identify themselves as such on census forms until 1961. Prior to that point they could choose Muslim as their religious affiliation but not as an ethnic identity. They then had to pick either Serb or Croat as an ethnic group. In 1953 the census allowed people to identify themselves as 'Yugoslavs-undeclared' for the first time. This provided an opportunity for Muslims to choose something other than Serb or Croat. In 1961, not only were people able to declare themselves ethnic Muslims, but the previous category of Yugoslav-undeclared was retained to capture people who held their state identity as their primary political identity.

This understanding of Muslim identity as *ethnic* rather than religious has made the Bosnian Muslim issue particularly difficult for outsiders to understand, as Bosnian Muslims do not fulfill stereotypes of what Muslims are. The threat of Islamic fundamentalism during the war in Bosnia was mostly imagined, as Islam had only lightly touched the Bosnian people and there were at that time few Muslim fundamentalists. Indeed, a 1985 survey in Bosnia reported only 17 per cent of Bosnians as holding any religious belief at all (Poulton, 1991: 109).

While the majority of Bosnian Muslims may not have been strong religious believers, Islam was still seen as threatening to the Yugoslav government. The leader of the Bosnian Muslim population from the early 1980s was Alija Izetbegovic. Izetbegovic gained recognition when he was tried along with 12 other Muslims for 'hostile and revolutionary acts derived from Muslim nationalism'.

Alija Izetbegovic

Born August 8, 1925, in Bosnia-Herzegovina, Alija Izetbegovic was the figurehead of the Bosnian Muslims during the entire latter half of the twentieth century. He received his B.S. in Law from the University of Sarajevo in 1956. His first brush with politics had happened during the Second World War, when he collaborated with the Nazi occupiers against Tito's communist regime. After the war, he was one of the leaders of the 1949 revolt against Tito. The revolt was unsuccessful and Izetbegovic was imprisoned for two years as a result.

Izetbegovic found himself in prison again from 1983 to 1988, on convictions for campaigning against what he perceived as the oppressive communist rule of Yugoslavia. In 1990, he founded the Party of Democratic Action in Bosnia. In the same year, his party defeated the communist party, making him President of Bosnia. As President, he led Bosnia through the war and was one of the signers of the Dayton Accord in 1995.

In 1996, Izetbegovic was re-elected President of Bosnia, along with a Serbian leader and a Croatian leader, as one part of a three-member collective presidency. However, in 2000, he stepped down, citing displeasure at the international community's minimization of the Islamic essence of Bosnia as his reason for doing so. On November 14, 2001, he was indicted at The Hague on charges of criminal responsibility for war crimes committed during the Bosnian War.

Muslims in Bosnia kept a rather low profile in terms of the public role of their religion. Muslims did not demand official recognition for Islamic holidays; their main newspaper, *Preporod*, remained informative as opposed to polemical; and Muslim leaders were not inflammatory or confrontational towards other ethnic groups (Ramet, 1996). Moreover, the form of Islam that developed in Bosnia was tremendously liberal when contrasted with the Wahabi Islamic practices that predominate in most of the Middle East. For example, many mosques in Bosnia allow both men and women to attend the mosque. Since 1986, female imams have been educated in Skopje and have been available to lead prayers for women in mosques.

In 1974 a new Yugoslav constitution was promulgated leading to a resurgence of nationalism. The new constitution responded to complaints of Serb chauvinism and control by transforming the centralized state into a more explicitly federal system of six ethnically-based republics: Serbia, Croatia, Bosnia-Herzegovina, Slovenia, Macedonia and Montenegro. The federalism answered some of the complaints of the non-Serbs in Yugoslavia. However, Serbs continued to dominate the Yugoslav National Army (JNA). Tito died in 1980 and during the decade that followed there was conflict within the regime between the Serbs, who wanted a stronger federal government, and the Slovenes and Croats, who wanted more devolved power.

This is reminiscent of the dispute that followed the establishment of the state in the wake of the First World War. After Tito's death the Yugoslav economy stagnated and some of the ethnic states began discussing the option of independence as a solution to the economic malaise. Slovenia and Croatia in particular, as the wealthiest of the states, thought that if they could achieve independence they could effectively integrate themselves with the economically prosperous Western Europe. These nationalist aspirations within Yugoslavia's richest areas created tensions in the state. Tensions remained into the post-communist period and were articulated along ethnic lines. After the fall of the Soviet Union, Croatia and Slovenia favoured independence and Serbia favored preserving the unity of the state.

THE RISE OF MILOSEVIC

Slobodan Milosevic, and other Serb leaders, portrayed Slovene and Croatian nationalist aspirations as anti-Serb. Beginning in 1984, Milosevic led the Belgrade branch of Serbia's Communist Party. He was elected president of the party in 1987. Through political means he succeeded in establishing Serbian control over the Albanian dominated province of Kosovo in 1989. That same year Milosevic was elected president of the Serbian Republic within Yugoslavia. Under Milosevic's leadership, the Communist Party transformed into the Serbian Socialist Party after the fall of the Soviet Union.

On June 28, 1989, several hundred thousand Serbs gathered near Pristina to commemorate the Battle of Kosovo. This was an annual cultural celebration for the Serbs, however, this particular year it turned into a political rally as well. Slobodan Milosevic gave a speech, appealing to the emotions of the crowd and fueling their sense of persecution and anger. This was an important event in the rise to power of Milosevic, because he effectively fomented Serbian nationalism and defined the interests of the Serbs *in opposition* to those of other ethnic groups in Yugoslavia. It also emphasized the fact that Milosevic had arrived. Not only did he command the votes of four of the eight states in Yugoslavia – Serbia, Vojvodina, Kosovo and Montenegro – due to their Serbian majorities, he also spoke for the nation. Serb nationalism was rising, and under the leadership of Milosevic it was antagonistic to other ethnic groups.

Not surprisingly, Croats, Bosnian Muslims and other ethnic groups within Yugoslavia also began to organize along ethnic lines around the same time. The Croats were led by Franjo Tudjman, a native Croat who had been actively opposing anti-democratic, communist and fascist forces since his imprisonment for anti-fascist activities in 1940 at the age of 18. Tudjman had been a general in the Yugoslavian Army. By the late 1980s he had retired from the army and in 1989 he started the Croatian Democratic Union (HDZ) through which he advocated for an independent Croatia. Tudjman also supported the Croatian forces within Bosnia.

In 1988 Izetbegovic was released from prison; and, in 1990, he began leading the Party of Democratic Action (SDA). By this time Bosnian Muslims were caught between Serb nationalism and a rising Croat nationalism. They were late to the game of ethnic mobilization and preparing for independence.

THE DISINTEGRATION OF YUGOSLAVIA

With the demise of the Soviet Union the glue that was in effect holding the Yugoslavian federation together disintegrated. Across the former Yugoslavia in 1990 elections were held to appoint new leaders for the post-communist era. In all of the regions, nationalists came to power. The election of nationalist leaders meant the pursuit of separatism was not far off.

Slovenia moved first for independence in 1990. The Yugoslavian National Army briefly attempted to fight to keep Slovenia within the union but the war was short and ineffective. Some argue that

Milosevic wasn't really committed to the conflict and was happy to see Slovenia go (Kaufmann, 2001: 191). Less than 70 people died fighting in the Slovenian war that only lasted a month.

The same year that Slovenia seceded from Yugoslavia, Bosnia had elections for the state presidency and assembly. These were the first truly free elections that Bosnia had ever experienced. The elections brought to power three ethnically defined nationalist parties that simply could not work together. The SDA led by Izetbegovic was the dominant party, but large minorities were won by the Serb Democratic Party (SDS), led by Radovan Karadzic and the Croatian Democratic Union (HDZ). The SDS was closely tied to the Serbian president Milosevic and the HDZ was closely tied to the Croatian leader Franjo Tudjman. The linkages between the political parties and other Yugoslav states made for tense relationships, particularly in the following year of 1991, when a Croatian declaration of independence led to the start of another war.

In the case of Croatia, the conflict was both more complicated and more gruesome than the previous war over Slovenia. Croatia was a multiethnic state; the majority of its population was Croatian, but Muslims and Serbs lived in the state as well. Croatia attempted to get rid of the Serbs within its police force by declaring them to be a protected minority and then removing them from duty. Trained Serb police officers who had lost their jobs organized paramilitary groups supported by Serbia to fight against Croatia. War began in the summer of 1991, lasting six months and resulting in approximately 10,000 deaths. The Croatian war ended in 1992 when Croatia received diplomatic recognition from Austria and Germany and when UN Forces intervened. When Croatia left the Yugoslav Federation, the future for Bosnia looked bleak due to the complicated ethnic composition of the state and the fact that Bosnian Serbs, Muslims and Croats had all been involved to some extent in the Croatian war.

The Croatian war was particularly threatening to Bosnia because in the past ethnic violence within Bosnia had often been triggered by external events. By 1992, politics within the Bosnian state were ethnically charged and divided. The interethnic balance within the Bosnian state that was established in the political institutions of the Tito era was gradually being dismantled by elites. The three nationalist parties representing the Croats, Serbs and Muslims were charged with eliminating the communists left in state administration, but they could rarely agree on whom to appoint in their place, resulting in a deadlock. Ethnic parties were able to fill open positions with their own members in areas where their support was the strongest.

1961–1991 per cent ethnic composition of Bosnia

	1961	1971	1981	1991
Serbs	42.8	37.3	32.2	31.4
Muslims	25.6	39.6	39.5	43.7
Croats	21.7	20.6	18.4	17.3
Yugoslavs	8.4	1.2	7.9	5.5
Montenegrins	0.4	0.3	0.3	
Albanians	0.1	0.1	0.1	
Slovenes	0.1	0.1	0.1	
Other	0.9	0.8	1.5	2.1*

* Includes three categories above
Source: (Woodward 1995)

While the war in Croatia was going on, and both politicians and citizens in Bosnia were anticipating a similar future, the ethnic groups within Bosnia began to prepare for war in a variety of ways. Serbs and Croats within Bosnia began to claim territory for themselves by forming autonomous regions that were free from the control of the central government in Sarajevo. The autonomous regions, or oblasts, comprised about three-fourths of the territory of Bosnia. The Bosnian government refused to conscript its own youth to fight for the Yugoslavian state against the Croat forces, yet Bosnian Serbs volunteered to fight against Croatia. Each of the three ethnic groups in Bosnia began to acquire weapons and train for armed conflict. The Yugoslavian National Army armed the Serbs (the army was still controlled by the Yugoslavian Federal government which meant *de facto* control by Milosevic). The Croats in Bosnia were being armed by Croatia. The Muslims in Bosnia were behind the curve in terms of the acquisition of weapons, yet they continued to train and organize, forming the Bosnian Muslim Green Berets. So the conflict in Croatia triggered the preparation of the three ethnic groups in Bosnia for armed conflict.

The UN arms embargo

On September 25, 1991, the UN Security Council imposed a 'general and complete embargo on all deliveries of weapons and military equipment to Yugoslavia' (UNSC Resolution 713). The embargo was directed at Croatia and Slovenia, as well as Serbia, Bosnia, Montenegro and Macedonia. The intent of the embargo was to decrease the amount of violence and the extent of the conflict that had broken out in the former Yugoslavia. However, the embargo was not effective for its original purpose because two of the three warring nations of the former

Yugoslavia – Serbia and Croatia – were already heavily armed. Indeed, the Serbs had at their disposal the Yugoslav National Army, a group of regulars that had been well-trained prior to the conflict. The effects of the embargo, therefore, fell predominantly upon the Bosnian Muslims. Though they were the largest ethnic group in Bosnia, the Muslims were the last group to mobilize for war and had little weaponry with which to counteract the attacks of the Serbs and Croats.

By 1994, it had become apparent that the arms embargo was affecting no one but the Bosnian Muslims. In November of 1994, the US decided that it would no longer participate in the enforcement of the embargo. Thus, it withdrew its ships from policing the waters along the coast of Bosnia. The following year, members of the Organization of the Islamic Conference (OIC) called for the lifting of the arms embargo, proposing instead that financial and weapons aid should be sent to Bosnia to aid the Muslims' self-defense. On November 22, 1995, the sanctions against the former Yugoslavia were indefinitely suspended. Overall, the arms embargo was ineffective, as it did not discourage war or harm all parties equally, but only adversely affected the Bosnian Muslims, which placed them at a disadvantage in regards to self-defense.

Meanwhile, no formal decision on Bosnian independence had been made. In January of 1992 in a debate held in the Bosnian assembly, it was decided that a referendum on independence should occur. The referendum occurred on February 29 and March 1 of 1992, and 63 per cent of the voters preferred independence to continued membership in the Yugoslav Federation. Many Serbs boycotted the vote. But how would the state be organized and who would control it?

Under the auspices of the European Union, negotiations were started immediately following the elections to establish the nature of Bosnia's future constitution, but the negotiations were futile as the three ethnic groups could come to no consensus. The only thing that was agreed upon was that each of the three ethnic groups would be able to control territory in which they had a majority of the population. The map that was drawn up by the European Community representatives brokering the talks was rejected by all sides.

UNPROFOR

UNPROFOR (the United Nations Protection Force) was initially established in February 1992 to facilitate demilitarization of the three zones in Croatia known as the 'United Nations

Protected Areas' (UNPAs). Additionally, the presence of the UN forces lent a sense of security to the people living in those regions of Croatia, as they could be confident in their defence from armed attack by the Yugoslav army. The mandate of the UN forces in Croatia was expanded to include the monitoring of entry into the UNPAs, the protection of humanitarian supply convoys and the distribution of those supplies.

Though based in Croatia, UNPROFOR was also responsible for the monitoring of the no-fly zones in Bosnia and Herzegovina as well as the UN-established safe areas around Sarajevo. When cease-fire agreements arose between the Serbs, Muslims and Croats in 1994–1995, the UN forces took on the duty of overseeing the implementation of those agreements. On March 31, 1995, the UN dismantled UNPROFOR in favour of a new plan involving three separate peacekeeping operations, which were somewhat interdependent but focused on more specialized operations than the broad mandate of UNPROFOR had allowed.

Figure 6.1 *Sarajevo.* ⓒ Stephanie Hirsh Montgomery

THE BOSNIAN WAR (1992–1995)

By mid-March, fighting had broken out in several cities across Bosnia-Herzegovina. The war began in April 1992, when Serbian forces from outside of Bosnia intervened in fighting that was occurring in the town of Bijeljina. On April 2 and 3, Serbian irregulars massacred the Muslim population of the town, incurring international outrage. On April 6, as the Serbs began shelling Sarajevo, Bosnia-Herzegovina was officially recognized as an independent state by the European Community and by the United States of America, however, independence was not recognized by the state of Yugoslavia.

As noted earlier, all sides in the conflict were prepared for the war. Arms had been flowing into Bosnia for the previous two years in preparation for conflict. In the beginning of the war, the fighting was primarily Serbs, supported by the Yugoslav army, against Muslims and Croats. However, by 1993, fighting had also broken out between Muslims and Croats, creating even more chaos. Muslims found themselves in the disadvantageous position of having control over a very small amount of territory in the centre of the country and a few enclave towns in the peripheral areas. This forced them to fight the Serbs and the Croats on multiple fronts.

Irregulars

All of the sides in the conflict relied on untrained soldiers outside of the normal chain of command (irregulars) as well as citizens and special units that made terrorizing the civilian population their primary goal. Arkan's Tigers (Serb) and the Black Swans (Muslim) were two of these gangs of irregulars who achieved notoriety for their violence against civilians. The use of irregular troops and civilians was typical of the Bosnian conflict, which some scholars have viewed to be an instance of post-modern warfare, due to the fact that both the primary targets and the primary combatants were civilians and the sides were defined on the basis of ethnicity (Kaldor, 1999).

Most people remember the Bosnian War for the particularly brutal nature of the 'ethnic cleansing' that occurred and, indeed, the introduction of the phrase ethnic cleansing into our vocabulary of warfare. Many civilians were killed in the Bosnian war, around 150,000. Yet, the numbers of other casualties and individuals affected is instructive. It is estimated that somewhere between 12,000 and 20,000 women were raped (Burg and Shoup, 1999: 170). Yet, as in the case of rapes reported during peacetime, this number is most likely substantially below the number of rapes that actually occurred. In addition, approximately half of the pre-war population of Bosnia-Herzegovina fled the country or was internally displaced. There are some differences in these figures based on ethnicity. Muslims encouraged their people to remain in their homes, while Serb and Croat leaders encouraged their populations to move to areas where they could be protected in the hopes of then maintaining control over those areas. In Bosnia, where the majority of the fighting took place during the conflict, there are still thousands of people unaccounted for, people that were displaced or killed as a result of ethnic cleansing.

Ethnic cleansing

The purpose of ethnic cleansing is to rid a certain territory of unwanted people. In the conflict in the Balkans, the principle behind ethnic cleansing was a ruthless desire for land that was either in the possession of the enemy or had inhabitants of the 'wrong' ethnic group. It happened on countless occasions. Though the Serbs were the most successful of the three major ethnic groups in the former Yugoslavia to use the method of ethnic cleansing as a tool of war, all sides used it to some degree.

All ethnic groups were the targets of ethnic cleansing, but the Serbs were less often the targets and more often the perpetrators. 'In the last analysis, given the number of Muslims expelled from Serb-controlled territory and the brutality that accompanied the expulsions, the sum total of atrocities committed by the Serbs was in a category by itself' (Burg and Shoup, 1999: 173). Ethnic cleansing and atrocities against civilians were particularly bad in Eastern Bosnia, so much so that this area became depopulated showing that ethnic-cleansing accomplished its goals.

The factor distinguishing all the groups in Bosnia is religion. Serbians are Eastern Orthodox, Croats are Roman Catholics and Bosnian Muslims are followers of Islam. Otherwise, all the people share a similar heritage. In Bosnia, religion signifies nationality and, as a result, religious institutions and symbols were targets of nationalist violence. This is one of the reasons why violence was channelled against mosques for destruction, clerics were deported and Muslim women were raped. Mosques, clerics and Muslim women all served as religious symbols, and religion formed the boundary of political identity.

At the end of 1994 there was no clear winning faction. The Serb area of Bosnia was depopulated because of the violence and Bosnian Serb leadership seemed unclear as to what path they should follow in the future. In the meantime, the Muslims and the Croats had declared a ceasefire and the Muslim led government was better off than it had been, though certainly not yet winning. The Serbs had also lost their desire to intervene, partly as a result of international condemnation and partly as a result of the rising domestic costs of intervention.

THE DAYTON AGREEMENT

Milosevic was clearly controlling the Bosnian Serbs from his position as the President of Serbia. Thus, it appeared very important to involve him in the process of trying to achieve an end to the fighting and a resolution of the conflict. In 1995, UNPROFOR's mandate expired and Croatian president Franjo Tudjman threatened not to support its renewal. This threat meant that some other international body or country would have to get involved, and the United States began to consider intervention in the war via a NATO operation. Since UN troops were being attacked by all sides, the UN withdrawal was virtually inevitable. The United States did not want to have to protect the UN troops as they withdrew and European allies seemed equally reluctant. In May of 1995, NATO became involved and began bombing Serb forces. Later on that year, the Croats launched a major offensive against the Serbs, followed by a Muslim offensive in the summer. The success of both of these operations seemed to mute Milosevic's desire to continue fighting in Bosnia. The American government's policy at that time was to use force and the threat of force against the Serbs alone and hope that over time the Croats and Bosnian government forces would make progress on the ground. NATO air attacks on Serbian positions were intended to bring the Serbs to the bargaining table. The air strikes were able to break the communications networks of the Bosnian Serbs and seriously impede their fighting ability.

The Serbs finally agreed to begin negotiations, but as a precondition, Slobodan Milosevic demanded recognition of a Bosnian Serb political entity within Bosnia called the Republika Srpska. Efforts to negotiate a cease-fire progressed through the fall of 1995. In November of that year the US was able to coerce the Serbs, Croats and Bosnian Muslims to the table in proximity talks held at a US Air Base in Dayton, Ohio. They successfully negotiated a peace agreement under the conditions of the Dayton Accord. The Dayton Accord put an end to the fighting and assured the peace in Bosnia through the presence of 60,000 NATO troops known as the Stabilization Force or SFOR. SFOR was intended to remain in place while the Bosnian political and economic infrastructure was rebuilt.

The Dayton Accord

The Dayton Accord created two entities within Bosnia-Herzegovina: The Federation of Bosnia-Herzegovina and the Republika Srpska. The Republika Srpska (RS) has distinct and clear political status and the right to establish independent relationships with neighbouring states. The government of

Bosnia-Herzegovina consists of a central state that is responsible for monetary policy, transportation, communications and air traffic control. The parliament has two houses. The House of Peoples has 15 delegates, 10 from the federation and 5 from the RS, confirming the ethnic divisions within the state. The second chamber is the House of Representatives with 42 members, 28 from the federations and 14 from the RS, all determined by direct election. Decision-making in both chambers is based on majority rule, but members of all ethnic groups are needed to assure a quorum, which essentially gives any one ethnic group the ability to block legislation. The presidency is composed of three members, one from each ethnic group, with the Serb elected from the RS and the Croat and Muslim from the federation. The constitution hammered out in Dayton is an attempt to promote power-sharing between the three ethnic groups, but whether this is the case remains to be seen.

When the Bosnian assembly ratified the Dayton Accord they put a time-limit on its implementation and determined that if it was not fully and quickly implemented the governing structure would revert back to the previous Bosnian governmental structure.

The conflict in Bosnia did not end with the Dayton Accord. It ceased to be demonstrated in terms of armed violence, but it continues to exist. There is still a very tenuous peace in Bosnia as the government has never been able to move beyond the structures of the Dayton Accord. Without the presence of SFOR troops it is likely violence would erupt again. It is unclear what the future for Bosnia will hold, as recent elections have assured the power of nationalist leaders rather than more politically moderate politicians.

PURSUING A LASTING PEACE

The Bosnian war led to the independence of Bosnia and a Yugoslavia composed only of Kosovo, Montenegro and Serbia. The war ended in 1995 and a conflict developed soon after in Kosovo as the Serbs tried to remove the Kosovar Albanians from Kosovo via a policy of ethnic cleansing.

In the 2000 elections, Milosevic lost the presidency. He did not want to resign his position and was forcibly removed from power after riots in Belgrade and replaced with Vojislav Kostunica. Kostunica tried to distance his regime from the aggressive Serbian nationalism of the Milosevic regime. Yet, there are pressing issues that remain as a result of the wars in Bosnia and later Kosovo. Among these issues is the fundamental problem of defining what Yugoslavia ought to be and whether it can be in any way multiethnic. In 1995 Russell Harding presciently observed that

> With Slovenia and Croatia out, being in Yugoslavia could no longer be appealing to the Muslims and Croatians of Bosnia. After the destruction of Bosnia, being in Yugoslavia could no longer be appealing to the non-Serbian majority populations of Kosovo and Macedonia. In the end even the Serbs may be uncomfortable in a Serbian Yugoslavia. (Hardin, 1995)

Hardin's observation could not have been more accurate. After the Bosnian war non-Serbs in Kosovo and Macedonia became concerned at what membership in Yugoslavia meant for them. In March 2002, Serbian President Kostunica supported a referendum to officially dissolve 'Yugoslavia' and make it Serbia and Montenegro. In May of 2002, the resolution passed. Yugoslavia no longer exists in Europe. It has been replaced by a loose federal union between Serbia and Montenegro. In three years even that may break down as there will be a referendum on independence for Montenegro.

CONSIDERING THE INTERNATIONAL DIMENSION

There is virtually no point in the history of the Bosnian conflict in which the role of outside states and interests was not critical. Once the state of Yugoslavia began to disintegrate in 1991, what were once domestic conflicts became international conflicts. The Croatian war for independence seemed to make the Bosnian War inevitable. Throughout the Bosnian War the conflict was fuelled by the neighbouring states of Croatia and Yugoslavia. One might argue that this was just an extension of the conflicts that began while all of these groups shared the same state. However, it is indicative of the problems that can result when conflicts over political identities take on an international character and spread to other states.

While the Bosnian conflict was fuelled by nearby states, it is the intervention of the United States and the NATO countries that ended the violence. While most countries did nothing to stop the war in the first few years, direct intervention through bombing, coupled with a push for a diplomatic solution, and the necessary mediation to achieve a negotiated settlement were all tactics employed eventually. By 1994, the international community began to take steps towards direct intervention as stories of the atrocities against civilians became widely publicized. Without international intervention, the war would almost certainly have continued for another year or more. Thus, both the causes and the solutions to the Bosnian war were international in nature.

APPLYING THE THEORIES

Is the Bosnian war best explained by primordial ethnic hatreds? Though the simple nature of this explanation is seductive, it is most likely untrue. Through most of history, relations between ethnic groups in the former Yugoslavia have been peaceful. The sudden development of ethnic hatreds can hardly be attributed to something primordial when it was absent for decades and then became present in a form strong enough to destroy a state. The general scholarly opinion is that there must be something else at work. Yet, among generalists there are some who remain unconvinced that ethnicity is *not* the crucial explanatory variable. Part of the reason this is the case is the role that conflict in the Balkans played in the First World War as well as the impact of a novel by Rebecca West published during the Second World War. The novel, *Black Lamb and Grey Falcon* (1941), is a beautifully written, romantic portrayal of Serbs within Yugoslavia which suggests radical and antagonistic differences between ethnic groups in Yugoslavia.

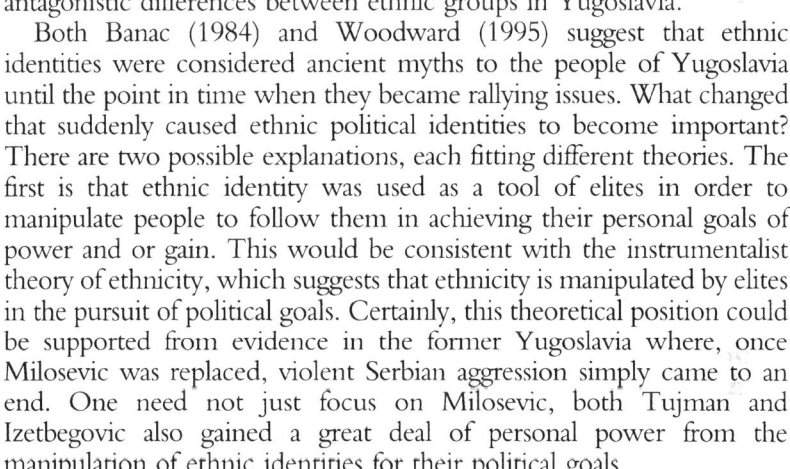

Both Banac (1984) and Woodward (1995) suggest that ethnic identities were considered ancient myths to the people of Yugoslavia until the point in time when they became rallying issues. What changed that suddenly caused ethnic political identities to become important? There are two possible explanations, each fitting different theories. The first is that ethnic identity was used as a tool of elites in order to manipulate people to follow them in achieving their personal goals of power and or gain. This would be consistent with the instrumentalist theory of ethnicity, which suggests that ethnicity is manipulated by elites in the pursuit of political goals. Certainly, this theoretical position could be supported from evidence in the former Yugoslavia where, once Milosevic was replaced, violent Serbian aggression simply came to an end. One need not just focus on Milosevic, both Tujman and Izetbegovic also gained a great deal of personal power from the manipulation of ethnic identities for their political goals.

The second explanation, consistent with the social constructivist position, is that the political and economic circumstances changed in such a way as to make the choice of an alternative identity to Yugoslavian compelling. The Soviet Union collapsed enabling Yugoslavia to renounce communism. The decline of communism then opened up the political arena for the expression of political identities that were not formed on the basis of ideology. It also enabled the potential for independent states to form and some potential states saw a great deal to be gained economically from renouncing the union. Once the Slovenes seceded from the Yugoslav Federation there was an inevitable spiral of war and secession resulting from years of suppressed nationalist sentiment and discontent with the policies of the Yugoslav federal government.

YOU DECIDE

Which theoretical perspective do you think best explains the rise in ethnic identities in Yugoslavia?
Does the presence of varied ethnic identities necessarily lead to violence?
What could be done to prevent the renewal of violence in Bosnia?
What was the role played by the various political leaders in the Bosnian conflict?

TIMELINE

1463 The Ottomans conquered the Balkans, bringing with them the religion of Islam.

1914 The First World War broke out in Serbia, with much of the fighting concentrated in the Balkans.

1944 Yugoslavian nationalist forces, led by Josip Broz Tito, pushed Germany out of Yugoslavia.

1948 Tito's communist regime declined an offer to merge with the Soviet Union.

1961 First census allowed Yugoslavians to ethnically identify themselves as 'Ethnic Muslim'.

1990 Yugoslavia's first free elections, in which the Communists were defeated by Serbian and Croatian national parties and a Muslim party from Bosnia-Herzegovina.

1991 Croatia and Slovenia both declared independence from Yugoslavia and set up their own parliaments, as did a multi-ethnic Bosnia-Herzegovina.

1992– Civil war broke in Bosnia-Herzegovina between the Bosnian
1995 Serbs, who were supported by Serbs from Serbia, Croats supported by Croatia and the Bosnian Muslims, who were in power at the time.

1995 The Dayton Accord divided Bosnia-Herzegovina into two separate states: the Muslim-Croat Federation of Bosnia & Herzegovina and the Republica Srpska.

1999 Violence breaks out in Kosovo against the ethnic Albanians living there.

2002 Yugoslavia ceases to exist. It is replaced by a loosely federated Serbia and Montenegro.

USEFUL WEBSITES

http://www.balkanpeace.org A thorough provision of data and media concerning the conflict in the former Yugoslavia, sponsored by the Centre for Peace in the Balkans.

http://www.its.caltech.edu/~bosnia/ Links to coverage of the conflict, including articles, photographs, and maps.

http://www.state.gov/www/regions/eur/bosnia/bosagree.html This site contains the text of the Dayton Accord, the signing of which formally ended the fighting in the Balkan region.

http://sipa.columbia.edu/REGIONAL/ECE/bosnia.html Information on Yugoslavia and the Bosnian conflict.

Bibliography

Burg, S.L., and Shoup, P.S. (1999) *The War in Bosnia-Herzegovina*. New York: M.E. Sharpe.

Burke, E. (1975) *Edmund Burke on Government, Politics and Society*. Edited by B. W. Hill. London: Fontana.

Hardin, R. (1995) *One for All*. Princeton, NJ: Princeton University Press.

Kaldor, M. (1999) *New and Old Wars*. Stanford, CA: Stanford University Press.

Malcolm, N. (1994) *Bosnia*. New York: New York University Press.

Poulton, H. (1991) *The Balkans: Minorities and States in Conflict*. London: Minority Rights Group.

Ramet, S.P. (1996) *Balkan Babel*. Boulder, CO: Westview Press.

West, R. (1941) *Black Lamb and Grey Falcon*. 1995 Reprint edn. New York: Penguin.

Woodward, S.L. (1995) *The Balkan Tragedy: Chaos and Dissolution After the Cold War*. Washington, DC: The Brookings Institution.

CHAPTER 7

Northern Ireland

Out of Ireland we have come.
Great hatred, little room,
Maimed us at the start.
I carry from my mother's womb
A fanatic heart.

[Yeats]

Northern Ireland, like Quebec, is an ethnic conflict that developed as the result of colonization. Ireland was colonized by the British in 1607, when the English and Scottish Protestants invaded the island, taking control of the land and turning the Irish peasants into tenants. In 1800, the British proclaimed the Union of England and Ireland. The Irish parliament was abolished and the Irish were given representation in the British parliament at Westminster. Later, in the nineteenth century, Ireland was struck by the potato famine.

The potato famine has had political repercussions that are manifest straight through to the present day. The large number of Irish descendents in the United States, Australia and the UK is a result of the potato famine. The famine was caused by a fungus that spoiled the potatoes, the staple food, while they were still in the ground. During the famine, which lasted from 1845 to 1850, the population dropped from 8 million to 5 million. One million people died from starvation, one million died from diseases such as cholera, typhoid and diphtheria which flourished due to unhygienic conditions, and one million emigrated. Unable to find food in the country, there was a rapid urbanization as people left for the towns and cities in droves. Recovery only began in the second half of the nineteenth century. As Ireland recovered, the demand for 'Home Rule', or independence from British control, grew.

The Easter Rising of 1916 punctuated the growing desire for Irish independence. The Rising was a revolt in Dublin that was supposed to be part of a nationwide uprising, but the plan was discovered before it spread. A small group of men decided to go ahead and launch a rebellion in Dublin in spite of the discovery. They took over the post office and led a week of street fighting. The Easter Rising was eventually crushed and the fifteen leaders of the revolt were taken into police custody and executed. Their deaths turned them into martyrs, and dissatisfaction with British occupation grew. By 1918 the majority of Irish members of the parliament at Westminster in London were demanding Home Rule. The Irish issue was becoming a difficult political issue for the Westminster parliament. Partly to rid themselves of an increasingly difficult political dilemma, the British devolved power to two regional parliaments, one in Northern Ireland and one in Southern Ireland, in the 1920 Government of Ireland Act. This intermediate political solution was not sufficient for the political desires of the south. Armed rebellion in that area resulted in the 1921 declaration of the Irish Free State. However, the Irish Free State came at a cost – the separation of six of the nine counties that made up the Irish region of Ulster. These six counties had Protestant majorities and did not want to be a part of an Irish state. Northern Ireland, sometimes referred to as Ulster, was to remain under the administrative structure of the government of Great Britain. This was a compromise between the British government, which wanted a solution to the independence issues, and the unionists of Northern Ireland – Protestant settlers and descendents of settlers – who wanted continued union with Great Britain.

Language

The use of language in any ethnic conflict is often contested and nowhere is there a better example of this fact than in Northern Ireland. There is a town in Northern Ireland called (officially) Londonderry. However, if you use that name you are a Protestant. Catholics don't call it that; they refer to the town as Derry. This is just a single example of the contested landscape of language in Northern Ireland. Within this chapter there are terms that are used to refer to the two separate sides, typically Catholic or Protestant. These terms are not meant to do anything but indicate which group is being discussed. However, there are multiple terms used to refer to both groups

Catholics – also called Nationalists, Republicans and even Greens
Protestants – also called Unionists, Loyalists and Orangemen (after William of Orange)

The creation of the territory of Northern Ireland was viewed as a solution to the demands for Irish Home Rule. The manner in which it was decided and implemented, however, was the cause of many future problems. Northern Ireland was left in a politically ambiguous position. It was supported politically and financially by the United Kingdom, but its specific responsibilities and the requirements of its parliament were unarticulated. This situation allowed the Northern Irish government to acquire some sovereignty but not full independence. Protestant Unionists sought more power, while parliamentarians in the London parliament were uninterested in further involvement. Disinterest in London was partially due to the size of Northern Ireland. Northern Ireland comprises only 3 per cent of the total population of the United Kingdom.

In 1921, Northern Ireland became independent in some matters: it had its own parliament, Stormont, its own civil service and its own security forces, but it still relied on the British state for funding. The British state did not supervise the parliament at Stormont closely, which allowed it to become infamous for its poor treatment of the Catholic minority. For example, one of the first acts of the Northern Ireland Parliament at Stormont was to change the voting rules and redraw local boundaries to make sure the Catholic minority could not gain political power. In 1967, as a result of this type of gerrymandering, in Londonderry County Borough 14,429 Catholic voters were represented by 8 non-Unionists, the remaining 8,781 Protestant voters were represented by 12 Unionist councillors (Arthur and 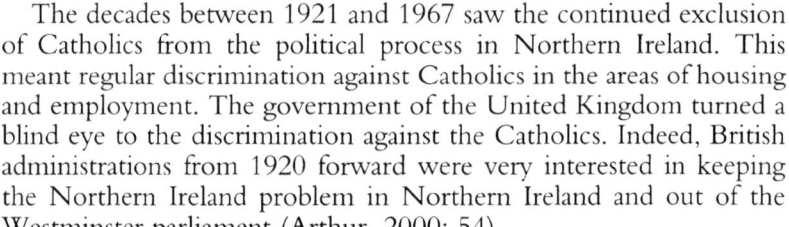 Jeffery, 1988: 5). Protestant Unionists manipulated political institutions in their favour with a predictability that amounted to the silencing of the large Catholic minority in Northern Ireland.

The decades between 1921 and 1967 saw the continued exclusion of Catholics from the political process in Northern Ireland. This meant regular discrimination against Catholics in the areas of housing and employment. The government of the United Kingdom turned a blind eye to the discrimination against the Catholics. Indeed, British administrations from 1920 forward were very interested in keeping the Northern Ireland problem in Northern Ireland and out of the Westminster parliament (Arthur, 2000: 54).

The issue of identity was contested and molded even during this time period. Many Protestants considered themselves to be English, not Irish, despite having lived on the island of Eire for generations. Catholics, on the other hand, defined themselves as Irish. This definition served two purposes: 1) it identified them as the original inhabitants of Ireland, 2) it indicated a solidarity and shared ethnic identification with the southern part of the island.

Voting rules

The Stormont parliament changed the voting rule from proportional representation to a first-past-the-post system in the first year that it was functioning. In a proportional representation system, the assembly is supposed to reflect the population. Thus, if 30 per cent of the people in Northern

Ireland vote for the Unionists, then 30 per cent of the seats should be held by Unionist politicians. Similarly, if 25 per cent vote for Republicans, then 25 per cent of the seats should go to Republican politicians and so on. Proportional representation is usually effected through the use of party lists whereby a voter votes for a party and the party then chooses candidates off its party list in order from the top of the party on down. First-past-the-post systems, such as those that exist in most of the UK and in the US, are winner-take-all elections in which it is not necessary for a candidate to win a certain percentage of the vote. The candidate with the largest number of votes wins. Thus, if there is a large minority and districting is controlled, it is possible to completely exclude the minority from the political process.

Political disintegration set in and peaked with the civil disobedience of the late 1960s and early 1970s. Civil disobedience was strongly influenced by the success of the Civil Rights Movement in the United States. The issues in both cases were similar, economic discrimination and exclusion from the political process. In 1967 the Northern Ireland Civil Rights Association was formed. It had five demands:

1 One man, one vote in local elections (as opposed to the system in place which allowed voting for 'businessmen and ratepayers' – the middle and upper class)

2 Changed electoral boundaries

3 Political mechanisms to deal with claims of discrimination

4 Fair housing

5 A disbanding of the Protestant auxiliary police force, the B specials which targeted Catholics for harassment

The civil disobedience that began in Northern Ireland was quite peaceful at first. Nevertheless, it turned violent and the British military was sent in to keep the peace. The first wave of British soldiers sent into Northern Ireland from 1969 to 1972 were operating under the orders of the Stormont parliament. Violence began and escalated in the urban areas as the Northern Ireland police and soldiers would crack down on demonstrators and the Catholic community would try and retaliate. Catholics began to feel very insecure in Protestant neighbourhoods and vice versa. People abandoned their homes in mixed neighbourhoods in order to feel more assured of their safety. Thus began the demographic division of Northern Ireland, and Belfast in particular, into Catholic and Protestant neighbourhoods.

Prior to the civil rights demonstrations of 1967–1969, the Irish Republican Army (IRA) had been inactive. Most people were not interested in it as it was not politically relevant to the average Catholic. The IRA had been operating an ineffective campaign along the border between Northern and Southern Ireland in the 1950s. The campaign targeted British troops and outposts, and succeeded in tormenting the British administration and capturing arms, but these were not the everyday concerns of the Catholic population in Northern Ireland. Support for the IRA declined through the 1950s and 1960s. Gerry Adams estimated that by 1961 there were only 24 IRA members in all of Belfast (Adams, 1996: 75). This is shocking even if it is an exaggeration.

Once the civil rights campaign began, many felt that the old, 'Official IRA' was too concerned with 'running seminars on Marxist theory than looking after their own' (Arthur and Jeffery, 1988: 37). As a result, the IRA split in 1970. The 'Provisional IRA' was younger, tougher, and advocated more intensive military campaign against the British administration. The Provisional IRA argued for a complete abstention from the political process until a unified Ireland was achieved. This inevitably meant a greater commitment to the use of violence to achieve a political voice. The Provisional IRA also wanted to organize to defend Catholic neighbourhoods in Belfast. This was this goal that successfully drew many Catholics to support its cause. The treatment of Catholic citizens of Northern Ireland went from bad to worse. Economic and political discrimination was compounded by a feeling of victimization by the security forces, which engaged in house searches and detained people without charge through the infamous policy of internment. Emerging stronger after the split, the Provisional IRA is the group we now commonly know as the IRA. The IRA is known, and even romanticized, for the incredible dedication and intensity of its members. At least one observer has noted that soon there may be more books and movies about the IRA than there are members (Hardin, 1995). The word 'Provos' is often used to refer to the IRA or to militant Catholics because of the 1970 split between the Provisional and the Official IRA. 'Provos' is used more generally because of the reference to the Provisional IRA as well as the Provisional nature of the British control of Northern Ireland.

On the Protestant side, militant organizations began forming by the late 1960s. The Ulster Volunteer Force (UVF) formed in 1966 and the Ulster Defence Association (UDA) followed in 1971. The UDA was an umbrella organization for all the Protestant groups that wanted to challenge the IRA militarily. It drew a tremendous amount of support from the outset. Though not as infamous as the republican IRA, the loyalist side has its own share of paramilitary groups. In addition to the UVF, which is the military wing of the Progressive Unionist Party (PUP), the Ulster Defense Association, which is associated with the Ulster Democratic Party (UDP), and the Red Hand Defenders, are two of the high profile groups. The leaders of these three paramilitaries combined – UVF, UDA and Red Hand – are known as the Loyalist Military Command.

The present 'Troubles' in Northern Ireland began in 1966, when the UVF declared war on the IRA and promised to execute its members mercilessly. That same year also saw the first deaths of the Troubles – all Catholic civilian victims of the UVF's terrorism.

In early 1972, the political climate in Northern Ireland changed for the worse. On Jan 30, 1972, 'Bloody Sunday', British soldiers shot dead 13 unarmed demonstrators in Derry. Outrage in the Irish Republic was so strong that the British Embassy in Dublin was burned to the ground.

Bloody Sunday

On January 30, 1972, the Northern Irish Civil Rights Association (NICRA) scheduled a protest march in Derry, Northern Ireland. Those marching were Catholics pushing for an end to the discrimination they faced in Northern Ireland. The march began at three in the afternoon, and a rally meeting was scheduled immediately following the march. After the protest, most people proceeded straight to the meeting, while some remained in the streets, heckling the local police. When it became apparent that they could not be calmed, the British Army arrived. According to statements by eyewitnesses, the British soldiers opened fire on the citizens as the latter were fleeing down the street, killing thirteen. Another man died soon thereafter from gunshot wounds. Seven of those shot and killed were under nineteen years of age, while a few of them were bystanders that had not been involved in the march to begin with. The incident inspired the hit song, *Sunday Bloody Sunday* by the popular Irish rock group U2.

An investigation soon after the events of that day, led by Chief Justice Widgery, absolved the British troops of all wrongdoing in the affair, claiming that they may have fired in self-defence. Despite this assertion, an examination of the site of the violence produced no evidence of bullets or bombs having been targeted at the soldiers. In 1998, the Bloody Sunday Inquiry was established by British Prime Minister Tony Blair in response to demands by the families of those injured and killed on that day that the facts be re-examined. The results of this current investigation, led by Lord Seville, are expected in 2004.

Reaction in London to Bloody Sunday was drastic and swift. The Stormont parliament was abolished and the government of the UK assumed direct rule of Northern Ireland. This put the Northern

Ireland issue right at the heart of British politics for every prime minister after 1972. The British government created a minister for Northern Ireland to serve in the cabinet and more troops were deployed, this time under the control of the UK government at Westminster. The presence of UK troops deployed by the government provided a target for the IRA and the violence began in earnest. The communities became polarized. Belfast was divided, with walls separating the neighbourhoods and people on both sides taking up arms. Internment, or incarceration without trial, began. Internment was one of the key rallying points of the Republican movement because it was so decidedly anti-democratic.

Internment

Internment means detention without trial. It was a policy used throughout the second half of the twentieth century in Northern Ireland to clamp down on Republican violence. After suspending Stormont, the Northern Irish regional parliament, in 1972 and adopting direct rule, the British increased the use of internment, arresting nearly 1,000 people. The overwhelming majority of these people were Catholics of Republican sentiment. It was not necessary to have any connection to the IRA to be interned; Catholic Republicans in general were targeted. After the British government agreed to hold talks with Sinn Fein in 1974, the interned prisoners were gradually released, so that by 1975, none remained.

All told, from August 1971 to December 1975, a total of 1,981 nationalists were detained without trial, while the number of loyalist detainees was only 107. Though the British have not employed the policy of internment in Northern Ireland since that time, they have continued to threaten its use. In the end, the policy did not achieve its goals; the evidence showed that there was no cessation of IRA violence during the implementation of internment. The brutal treatment of interned prisoners served rather to inspire more violence in Northern Ireland as people reacted to the violations of civil rights.

Throughout the 1970s and 1980s, the Troubles continued. Young people living in the Protestant and Catholic communities of Northern Ireland became radicalized by the violence, adding to the recruits for paramilitaries on both sides. Through violence, the paramilitaries on both sides were able to command a tremendous amount of attention to their causes. However, they were not the only voices. Catholics were represented by the Social Democratic Labour Party – SDLP, which consistently won between 15 and 25 per cent of the total vote in Northern Ireland in the 1970s and 1980s. They support the unification with Ireland, but only in the long term. They have not supported the use of violence as a political tool. However, Sinn Fein, the political wing of the IRA, has supported violence and political abstention as forms of protest. Before the cease-fire in 1994, Sinn Fein was so unpopular it could not win representation in parliament even in districts that had a majority of Catholics. Gerry Adams, President of Sinn Fein, held the only seat Sinn Fein ever won in the London Westminster parliament. Sinn Fein and the IRA illustrate an interesting point. For all of their political influence, the IRA had little support from the Catholic population until they adopted the cease-fire. Though many Catholics may have been sympathetic to the cause of the IRA, they were apparently not sympathetic with the violence used in support of the cause.

Gerry Adams

Gerry Adams was born on October 6, 1948, in the working-class neighbourhood of West Belfast. He joined Sinn Fein as a teenager in the 1960s – a time when tensions were heating up between Protestants and Catholics in Northern Ireland. In 1972, he was interned without trial by the British on the prison ship Maidstone and was imprisoned again from 1973 to 1977. Adams was elected Vice President of the Provisional Sinn Fein in 1978 and President of the party in 1983. That same year, he was elected to the British Parliament representing West Belfast, though he refused to take his seat rather than make the compulsory oath of allegiance to the British Queen Elizabeth II.

As leader of Sinn Fein, Adams' secret talks with fellow republican John Hume, leader of the Social Democratic and Labour Party (SDLP), were instrumental in leading to the IRA ceasefire announcement in 1994. Though many believe him to have been a former IRA member himself, Adams has denied any involvement with the Republican paramilitary group. Over the years, he has emphasized the expression of Northern Irish Republican opinion through the vote rather than violence.

Adams survived an assassination attempt by loyalist para-militaries in 1984, but was severely wounded by the attack. He has been extremely influential in the shaping of Sinn Fein policy in his tenure as President. He was recently reelected to Westminster in 2001, winning 66.1 per cent of the vote in his West Belfast constituency.

On the Protestant side the political party that has always carried the majority of the Protestant vote is the Ulster Unionist Party (UUP). They have led every parliament under the old Stormont administrative structure and are currently the majority party in the Northern Ireland Assembly. The UUP position has historically been in support of direct rule from Britain with no devolution to the region. However, they have amended this position since 1998 and are now more conciliatory under the leadership of David Trimble.

David Trimble

David Trimble was born in Northern Ireland in October, 1944. He attended Queen's University in Belfast, after which he became a barrister in addition to a lecturer at his *alma mater*. His first involvement with politics was with the Vanguard Party in the 1970s, a hard line Unionist group. The year 1978 marks his shift to a mainstream Unionist ideology, and in 1992 he became the Westminster MP representing the district of Upper Bann in Northern Ireland. After winning leadership of the Ulster Unionist Party in 1995, he made enemies on both sides of the Unionist/Nationalist line when he negotiated with Sinn Fein to forge the Good Friday Agreement – for which he shared the Nobel Peace Prize with John Hume of the SDLP in 1998. He then became First Minister of Northern Ireland under the terms laid out in the Good Friday Agreement, a position he resigned in 2001 as a result of the IRA's refusal to decommission its weapons. After the IRA began to decommission later in the year, Trimble was reelected as First Minister, but not without difficulty, as several Unionist factions refused to support him.

Protestants are also represented by the Democratic Unionist Party (DUP), led by the Reverend Ian Paisley. The DUP is staunchly loyalist, against any sort of power-sharing arrangement with the Catholics.

In response to the growing violence and apparent lack of solutions in Northern Ireland, the UK and Irish governments agreed to the Anglo-Irish Accord in 1985. The Accord involved the Republic of Ireland in consultation on solving the Troubles. Margaret Thatcher, then prime minister of the UK, agreed to negotiate directly with Dublin regarding the future of Northern Ireland. This made the Protestants furious, but it was tremendously important. It was unique because the accord recognized the Republic of Ireland, a completely separate state, as a major player in Northern Irish politics for the first time, and then gave them a role in bringing about a solution.

Recognition of the role of Ireland in the Anglo-Irish Accord left the Unionists feeling betrayed. The Unionists – particularly the Ulster Unionist Party, which had been a majority in the Northern Ireland assembly at Stormont since it was formed – were furious that the Republic of Ireland was being consulted on Northern Irish affairs. They saw it as the first step in the UK abandoning sovereignty over Northern Ireland. Only time will tell if that opinion was true; what is clear is that this agreement completely changed the power relationships within Northern Ireland. The Protestant Unionists could no longer count on the UK government for unquestioning support, and the Catholics had an ally in their pursuit of basic civil rights.

The 1985 Anglo-Irish Accord set the stage for the negotiation of a cease-fire and the eventual prospect of peace by pitting both the Irish and English governments against the armed political groups in Northern Ireland. The political opening created by the Anglo-Irish Accord languished through the late 1980s, but took life again in the 1990s, particularly after a swing toward a Labour government in the UK meant that the votes of the UUP members in the Westminster parliament were no longer so influential. During the Major administration (1990–1997) a very slim Conservative majority was achieved with the cooperation of UUP members, who always courteously voted with the Conservative government as long as that government continued to support their cause in Northern Ireland.

In spite of this political difficulty, in the early 1990s the Major administration began secret talks with both Sinn Fein and the SDLP. Increased violence in Northern Ireland made a new political initiative imperative. The violence, much of it random in nature, increased both the fear and the political pressure in Protestant and Catholic communities alike. Moreover, there was a military stalemate. The IRA had proven it could resist British efforts to eliminate it. The British had proven their commitment to retaining control.

In December of 1993 the prime ministers of the UK and The Republic of Ireland made a joint declaration that if the IRA decommissioned its weapons, Sinn Fein would be invited to talks on the future of Northern Ireland. The Downing Street Declaration, as it was called, also affirmed that the British government would not abandon Northern Ireland without the consent of its people. Then, in January 1994, against the advice of all of his advisors, Bill Clinton ordered that Gerry Adams be granted a visa to come to the United States for a speaking engagement. This action was highly symbolic and encouraged the new efforts at inclusion of all parties in the Northern Irish peace process.

In August 1994, the IRA declared a cease-fire, followed shortly thereafter by a loyalist paramilitary cease-fire. In 1996, after a brief violation of the cease-fire by the IRA, elections were held to designate the parties which could take part in the peace process. A framework

117

document articulating the basis for agreement was negotiated. Three mediators external to the process were brought in, including former US Senator George Mitchell. During several months of negotiations, which included political parties from both sides, even those representing the paramilitaries, the Good Friday agreement was hammered out.

The Northern Ireland Women's Coalition

The Northern Ireland Women's Coalition (NWIC) was founded in the spring of 1996 by Monica McWilliams as a means of increasing women's participation in the multi-party Peace Talks that were taking place at the time. The political agenda of the NWIC is non-sectarian; its goals are 'reconciliation through dialogue, accommodation and inclusion' as well as raising the participation of women in politics. As a result, the party attracts women from a wide variety of Northern Ireland's political traditions, including Unionists, Nationalists, Loyalists and Republicans, all of whom unite under the flag of human rights, inclusion and equality.

The NWIC currently has two representatives sitting in the Northern Irish Assembly. Monica McWilliams was the only female signatory of the Good Friday Agreement in 1998 and was elected that same year from the constituency of South Belfast. Jane Morrice has represented County Down since 1998 and was elected Deputy Speaker of the Northern Irish Assembly in 2000.

THE GOOD FRIDAY AGREEMENT

Known alternately as the Belfast Agreement or officially as The Framework Agreement Reached in the Multi-Party Negotiations, the negotiated accord is called the Good Friday Agreement because it was voted on in Northern and Southern Ireland on Good Friday 1998. The document was intended to be valid if supported by the majority of people in both Ireland and Northern Ireland. It achieved this and more. As part of the agreement, the Republic of Ireland agreed to amend its constitution and renounce any claim to Northern Ireland. The territorial claim to Northern Ireland which was present in articles 2 and 3 of the Irish constitution were dropped and replaced by an 'aspiration' to unite the peoples of Ireland. When the voting came, the Republic of Ireland gave a huge majority (94 per cent) to a 'yes' vote on the implementation and there was also a majority, though not as substantial, in Northern Ireland (71 per cent).

The agreement has three fundamental thrusts: 1) acceptance by the Nationalists or Republicans of the present position of Northern Ireland within the UK, 2) power-sharing between the Catholic and Protestant populations, 3) links to the Republic of Ireland. There are several specific areas in which the Good Friday Agreement has made tremendous advances in bringing about a solution to the violence and the problems of political representation.

Power-sharing between the two communities

Power-sharing now occurs in Northern Ireland at two levels: the executive level and the legislative level through the assembly. It was clear to everyone that whatever agreement was negotiated had to contain a vehicle for power-sharing in both the executive and within the parliament itself. George Mitchell, the former US Senator and special envoy to Northern Ireland noted that 'even the dogs in the street knew that without a power-sharing executive in place, there would be no decommissioning [of weapons]' (O'Malley, 2001: 277). Power-sharing within the assembly occurred through a system of proportional representation and veto power for the minority community (now the Catholics but perhaps the Protestants at some point in the future). Key decisions need a weighted majority of at least 40 per cent of the votes from each community in the assembly. Members of the assembly must declare their Unionist or Republican perspective. Moreover, the assembly is unique in that it has the specific responsibility to implement the requirements of the Good Friday Agreement, including the decommissioning of weapons held by the paramilitary groups. This has been one of the stumbling blocks of complete implementation of the accord due to the fact that there has been a great reluctance on the part of the paramilitaries to disarm.

Shared sovereignty between Ireland and the United Kingdom

The Good Friday Agreement established the North–South Ministerial Council. The North–South Ministerial Council is composed of representatives of the Northern Ireland Assembly as well as representatives from the parliament of the Republic of Ireland. It is specifically empowered to address issues of interest to both Northern and Southern Ireland such as language, agriculture, tourism and environment. The North–South Ministerial Council is a completely unique institution because it awards decision-making power to the Republic of Ireland in British territory – something quite new. It is meant to ensure the long-term and constructive involvement of the Republic of Ireland in the affairs of the North.

Civil Rights Protections

The Good Friday Agreement established a human rights commission and outlawed any sort of discrimination based on group identity or religious beliefs. It also legislated attempts to address pre-existing inequalities in the police and civil service. The fact that the police force was almost entirely Protestant was viewed as a tremendous barrier to peace. As long as the police are not fully integrated they are not viewed as the protectors of all citizens, making them a potential target for violence.

The Good Friday Agreement gives strong protections to both communities, but does not eliminate the potential for conflict. A critical component of this and all recent agreements on Northern Ireland is the British position that if a majority of the population decide that they want to be part of Ireland then that will happen. With an increasing Catholic population that situation seems likely to be a realistic possibility at some point in the not so distant future. What then will Northern Ireland Loyalists do? Will they quietly accede to be a part of the Irish state? It is unclear. Protestants do not want to end up as an oppressed religious minority in Ireland, which is essentially the status of Catholics in Northern Ireland now. At a subconscious level there is a fear of retribution, a fear of becoming the Catholics, becoming what they have oppressed.

The Revenge of the cradle

The official position of the British government towards nationalist sentiment in Northern Ireland has always been a democratic one. According to the UK government, if a majority of citizens in Northern Ireland favour secession, then the territory may secede. Over the past couple of decades, Protestant Unionists in Northern Ireland have had reason to worry for the future of the union, as the Catholic Nationalist population in Northern Ireland is increasing rapidly. Here there truly is a revenge of the cradle.

At the time of the split of the Irish island in 1920, Roman Catholics made up about one-third of the population of Northern Ireland. The figures were similar in 1971, when Roman Catholics accounted for 31.4 per cent of Northern Ireland's population. Ten years later, in 1981, the figure was down slightly to 28.0 per cent. The census of 1991 illustrates a large leap in the Roman Catholic population, now composing

41.5 per cent of the population of Northern Ireland. Projected figures from the 2001 Census estimate a rise to 45 per cent. At this rate, it is quite possible that Roman Catholics will be the majority population in Northern Ireland in a matter of decades, a fact which has incredible political ramifications.

Since the signing of the Good Friday Agreement violence has not completely ended, but it is much reduced. There are still riots and outbursts of sectarian violence, but these have not been sustained. The conflict that exists has moved into the political sphere and off the streets. The success of the Good Friday Agreement has been its ability to keep peace and to give hope for a political solution where previously no such hope existed. However, the underlying conflict still exists. On numerous occasions since the Good Friday Agreement, the ability of the assembly to implement the accord has been questioned. Indeed, the Northern Ireland Assembly ceased to function on several occasions because of conflict over the decommissioning of weapons by the IRA.

Decommissioning of weapons has been one of the most troublesome issues for the assembly to deal with because, like all important political issues in Northern Ireland, it is laced with questions of equity and the long-term security of the communities. The IRA made an agreement to decommission its weapons in order to win the participation of Sinn Fein in the multi-party negotiations that preceded the Good Friday Agreement. The IRA began decommissioning its weapons on October 2001, monitored by an international arms body, which described the number of weapons as 'significant'. On April 9, 2002, the IRA put even more weapons out of commission, in order to prove to Unionists that they remain committed to the peace process and that the first act was not a 'stunt'. The IRA claims that all of its weapons will be decommissioned by May 2003.

ANALYSIS

One of the most interesting aspects of the conflict in Northern Ireland is that it is an ethnic conflict articulated in religious terms, yet the conflict is not over religion. The conflict between the Catholics and Protestants in Northern Ireland is over the issue of sovereignty. In Northern Ireland, Catholics are not and were not demonstrating in the streets for the right to attend mass, practice the sacraments, etc. The political issue is *not* religion, it is political sovereignty – which group will control the territory.

121

The dispute over sovereignty in Northern Ireland is referred to as a bicommunal conflict – two groups are competing over the same territory. In the case of Northern Ireland, the two communities exist in relative isolation. It is possible for a Protestant child to grow up in Belfast in a Protestant neighbourhood, go to Protestant schools, play sports with other Protestant children and eventually go to university with other Protestants. Adults segregate themselves by religion in their social activities, the pubs at which they drink and the clubs they join. It is possible for Protestant and Catholic children to grow up in Northern Ireland with very little contact with the 'other' community. This isolation of the communities began with the start of the Troubles when living among members of the other group was dangerous due to the fighting; it began as a manifestation of the need for security.

There have been various attempts by groups interested in conflict resolution to try and address the isolation of the two communities. The belief is that if children and adults meet people from the other community they will be less likely to view the other community in its entirety as enemies. One of the oldest and most well-known organization that has been working to overcome the barriers between the two communities is the Corrymeela Community.

Corrymeela Community

The Corrymeela Community is an ecumenical reconciliation group that works with both Protestants and Catholics in Northern Ireland. Corrymeela, 'hill of harmony' in Gaelic, was founded in 1965 by Ray Davey, a Second World War veteran. Among the early goals of the Community were training Christian laymen/women to play a responsible part in the church and society, bringing people together in Christian fellowship through work camps and providing a place where reconciliation can happen, both within the church as well as in the wider community

The goals of the Corrymeela Community have changed over time as the group has adapted to changes in the political landscape of Northern Ireland. The Community now owns and operates several facilities in Northern Ireland, where people suffering from trauma or stress due to the unrest can find shelter and support. Also among its work is educating the public regarding the history of the conflict, in order to minimize the types of prejudices that stem from ignorance. The Corrymeela Community continues in its reconciliation endeavours by holding integrated summer camps for young people and seminars for adults.

The efforts of the Corrymeela Community and other organizations engaged in similar activities are critical to achieving long-term peace in Northern Ireland. In order for the conflict in Northern Ireland to be successfully concluded, there must be an agreement between the two communities to refrain from violence. The two communities have to move from being enemies to working together as a 'security community', what Karl Deutsch refers to as a set of relationships where there is 'a real assurance that the members of the community will not fight each other physically, but will settle their disputes in some other way' (Arthur, 2000: 16). Ultimately, the hope for peace rests on the success of this endeavour.

One of the ways to measure the degree to which two groups view each other as enemies is to examine the rates of intermarriage between them. In the case of Northern Ireland the statistics are interesting. Though we do not have data from all the years of the conflict, from the data below we can see that intermarriage rates have tripled since 1988. This bodes well for the future as it appears to indicate that people are interacting with the other religious group and that they are willing to join families with the other community.

Mixed Marriage Rates in Northern Ireland

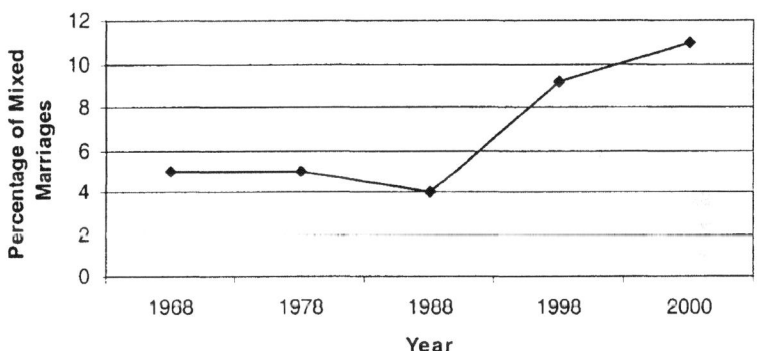

Figure 7.1 *Mixed Marriage rates in Northern Ireland*

Sources: Cairns, Ed. 'The Role of the Contact Hypothesis in Peacemaking in Northern Ireland: From Theory to Reality'. Found at: http://construct.haifa.ac.il/~cerpe/papers/cairns.html
Cadwallader, Anne. 'Mixed Couples defy decades of Northern Irish Discord', *The Christian Science Monitor*. Dec. 13, 2001. Found at: http://www.csmonitor.com/2001/1213/pls4-woeu.htm

This graph is encouraging. People who choose a spouse from another community will not be able to live in isolation, nor will their children.

CONSIDERING THE INTERNATIONAL DIMENSION

Ireland was the first colony ever established by Britain and that colonial legacy created a psychology of subordination among Irish leaders. They did not see themselves as being on an equal footing with the British until the latter part of the twentieth century. The development of the European Economic Community and its successor the European Union changed all that. Within the European Economic Community and the European Union, Ireland had an equal voice to that of the United Kingdom. Ireland has expanded its international role and its economy has been vibrant and growing while the opposite has been true in both cases for the UK. A growing international role for Ireland opened up the possibility that it could become a serious player in the solution to the Northern Ireland conflict. As political alternatives were developed in the 1990s, Ireland became an active participant.

The United States also played an important role in bringing about the conditions in which the Good Friday Agreement could be negotiated and implemented. During his administration, US President Bill Clinton tried to encourage a resolution to the Troubles, albeit in ways that were controversial – such as granting Gerry Adams a visa to come to the United States. Once the multi-party talks had started, the Clinton administration sent former Senator George Mitchell to moderate the talks. Mitchell was able to revive the talks and with great patience and skill, bring the Ulster Unionists and Sinn Fein to agreement on procedures and, ultimately, on the text of the Good Friday Agreement.

International involvement was extremely important in facilitating attempts by the government of the United Kingdom to bring peace to Northern Ireland. The roles played by both the Republic of Ireland and the United States helped to give legitimacy to the peace process and to push it along when it otherwise might have stalled due to the rancorous disagreement between the opposing sides.

APPLYING THE THEORIES

As with the other chapters, in this section we will try to apply the theories that we have discussed throughout the book as a framework for understanding the nationalist conflict that we see in Northern Ireland.

Primordialism

Primordialism is the theoretical school that suggests that ethnic identities are with us from birth and are unchangeable. Primordialists would suggest that ethnic conflict would be inevitable in a case such as Northern Ireland because you have two distinct peoples, the English and the Irish, competing for control of the same territory. This conflict is ultimately rooted in the English colonization of Ireland. The fact that many people who consider themselves English remain in Northern Ireland is a remnant of the colonial era when many English Protestant settlers came from England to Ireland. Now, generations later, some still consider themselves to be English. This type of identification with an ethnic homeland, and the role of historic origins in the political reality of the present day, is something that primordialism helps us to understand. However, there are also a large number of Protestants in Northern Ireland who consider themselves to be Irish. As the first Protestants came to Ulster in the 1500s, this should not be surprising. Catholics tend to consider themselves to be Irish, but Protestants could consider themselves to be either English or Irish, so the terms 'Catholic' and 'Protestant' are more often used to define the sides in the conflict.

Primordialism is less helpful in explaining why the conflict has been articulated so often as Protestant versus Catholic. Primordialists believe ethnic identities to be fixed at birth. While it is possible to make a strong case for English and Irish identities being fixed, it is virtually impossible to do so for religious identities that can be changed by choice and practice. Religious identities are what we refer to as achieved characteristics – they can be changed during a person's lifetime. Thus, primordialism cannot convincingly explain why a conflict would be articulated in these terms.

Instrumentalism

Leaders use ethnic identities to achieve personal or communal goals – or so instrumentalists believe. In order to apply instrumentalism to the conflict in Northern Ireland, we need to examine the goals of the leaders and the practices they follow to determine whether or not they are manipulating ethnicity to pursue some personal end. On the Unionist/Protestant side of the conflict there seems to be a convincing amount of evidence for this interpretation, particularly in the role of the Stormont parliament. As soon as power was devolved to the Stormont parliament in 1921, they set about trying to exclude the Catholic community from having a political voice. This effectively put Protestant leaders and the Protestant community in a superior position. They were able to use the political system to pursue the goals of the group and individual Protestant leaders were empowered by the exclusion of the Catholics. The Stormont parliament is infamous among Catholics for the exclusionary nature of politics while it was in power. This exclusion clearly benefited the Protestant community.

However, instrumentalism is less persuasive from the Catholic/ Nationalist side of the conflict. It is difficult to see what benefit individual Catholics gained from leading the struggle. The Troubles began in 1968, and it was not until 30 years later that Catholic leaders were able to gain a legitimate political voice in Northern Ireland. Prior to that point in time, they were subject to imprisonment without trial and, in the early years of the Troubles, this happened to those that opposed the use of violence as well as those that supported it. The aggressive response of the British government, coupled with the maintenance of a first-past-the-post electoral system with gerrymandering, ensured no strong Catholic voice in democratically elected leadership and retribution for those that espoused violence. Given this set of incentives for leaders, it is difficult to ascertain what sort of benefits the leaders of the Catholic Nationalist movement would gain. Even if they expected benefits in the early years of the Troubles, certainly they would have learned after ten or fifteen years that their personal benefits would be limited.

Social Constructivism

Social constructivists argue that it is political and economic circumstances combined with some element of ascribed identity that form ethnic identities. In the case of Northern Ireland this theory explains both sides of the conflict. On both sides there is some element of ascription. Protestants, whether they consider themselves Irish or English, can identify their origins in Northern Ireland as a result of the colonization of the island. Moreover, on both sides of the conflict, political gains and economic inequalities have fuelled ethnic identification and the bicommunalism that developed over time. Catholic unemployment and economic inequality was never addressed politically because power was concentrated in the hands of the Protestant politicians who refused to do so. As a result the Catholics had a political grievance. When the Troubles began, the two sides saw the conflict as a zero sum gain – a win for one side was a loss for the other and vice versa. This set of political and economic circumstances fostered grievances between the two communities, which turned violent during the Troubles. The peace that exists currently is due to the changed the political and economic circumstances, and incentives that have been developed as a result of the Good Friday Agreement.

YOU DECIDE

Which theory do you think best explains the conflict in Northern Ireland?
What is the role of religion in forming ethnic identity? Does changing your religion change your ethnic identification?
Is violence ever justified in seeking resolution to political problems?

TIMELINE

1649 Oliver Cromwell, invades and conquers Ireland.
1690 William of Orange defeats James II at the Battle of the Boyne. This victory is celebrated today by Unionists in Northern Ireland on July 12.
1916 The Easter Rising.
1920 Government of Northern Ireland Act created an autonomous area in Southern Ireland in the southern part of the island, while the Ulster counties in the north remained under British control. Both parts of the Irish island have their own parliaments, but both are still subordinate to Westminster.
1921 Anglo-Irish treaty supercedes the act of the previous year, and Ireland is granted political independence.
1968 A civil rights march is held in Derry on October 5. It was stopped by the RUC (Royal Ulster Constabulary), and many people were injured in the fray, including several MPs. This date is seen as the start of the Troubles.
1969 In December, the IRA splits, with the splinter group becoming the Provisional IRA, with the remaining group being called the Official IRA.
1972 The British Army shoots 13 people to death during a civil rights march in Derry on January 30, 'Bloody Sunday'. The British government imposed direct rule on Northern Ireland.
1985 The Anglo-Irish Agreement was forged between Britain and the Republic of Ireland, in which England agreed to confer with the government of the Republic on all matters concerning Northern Ireland. Northern Irish Unionist MPs resigned their seats at Westminster in protest.
1993 England and Ireland jointly issue the Downing Street Declaration. It proclaimed the right to self-determination for citizens in both parts of Ireland.
1994 On August 31, a ceasefire is declared by the Provisional IRA.
1998 Good Friday Agreement signed.

USEFUL WEBSITES

http://www.bbc.co.uk/history/war/troubles Comprehensive information on most of the events related to the Troubles.

http://www.usip.org/library/pa/ni/nitoc.html Text of the Good Friday Agreement.

http://www.niwc.org/ Homepage of the Northern Ireland Women's Coalition, containing party information and biographies of its leading figures.

http://cain.ulst.ac.uk/ni/popul.htm University of Ulster index to the Northern Ireland conflict.

Bibliography

Adams, G. (1996) *Before the Dawn*. New York: William Morrow and Company, Inc.

Arthur, P. (2000) *Special Relationships: Britain, Ireland and the Northern Ireland Problem*. Belfast: The Blackstaff Press.

Arthur, P., and Jeffery, K. (1988) *Northern Ireland since 1968*, edited by A. Seldon. London: Basil Blackwell.

Hardin, R. (1995) *One for All*. Princeton, NJ: Princeton University Press.

Mitchell, G. (2001) *Making Peace*. Berkeley, CA: University of California Press.

O'Malley, P. (2001) 'Northern Ireland and South Africa: "Hope and History at a Crossroads"', in *Northern Ireland and the Divided World*, edited by J. McGarry. New York: Oxford University Press.

Yeats, W.B. (1974) 'Remorse for Intemperate Speech', in *The Collected Poems of W.B. Yeats*. New York: Macmillan.

CHAPTER 8

Eritrea

*As genocide represents the ultimate breakdown in civil society, so territorial
dismemberment entails the final failure of a nation-state.*

[Young, 1986]

Eritrea is one of the youngest states in the world. It has formally
existed only since 1993, yet, the origins of the state date back to the
era of the colonization of Africa. Like both Quebec and Northern
Ireland, in Eritrea the colonization of the country by the Italians set
the stage for a long political conflict and for competing ethnic and
political identities. However, unlike Quebec and Northern Ireland,
the ethnic group that was created in Eritrea through colonization
became a nationalist movement that was ultimately successful in
achieving a separate state.

It is not unusual that three of the four cases studies in this book
discuss ethnic conflicts that became nationalist movements as a result
of the political remnants of the colonization process. Colonization, by
virtue of the fact that it established political boundaries that cut across
pre-existing ethnic groups, brought new languages and political
structures and often favoured certain groups over others, creating an
entirely new landscape of competing interests. When colonizing
powers left, their legacy was often one of conflict and competition.
This was the case in Africa and the Indian subcontinent as well as in
North America. Colonialism had an impact that is felt throughout the
world to this day.

Virtually the entire continent of Africa was colonized by Western
powers in the later half of the nineteenth century. Only Ethiopia and
Liberia were untouched by European rule. Though France and Great
Britain controlled the vast majority of the African continent, other
European countries such as Belgium, Portugal and Italy were also
involved. The Italians colonized Eritrea. Italian colonization in Eritrea
left a mixed legacy. The Italians constructed a beautiful city in Asmara
the Eritrean capital. With its wide boulevards, beautiful white stone
houses and flowering bougainvillea, Asmara is a jewel of a city. Yet the
Italians also left a people with a unique historical experience that was
the basis for a separate ethnic identity and 'ultimately' a nationalist
movement of great force.

Eritrea is included in this book as a case study because it is relatively
unusual in two regards: 1) it is a nationalist conflict that successfully

achieved its goals of a separate state, 2) it illustrates how ethnic identities can be created over time and become so important that people are willing to sacrifice their lives for that identity. Eritrea was created out of a long fought struggle for independence in which many people lost their lives so that the nation could have a state.

ERITREAN POLITICAL HISTORY

Eritrea is located in the Eastern part of Africa in an area referred to as the Horn of Africa because it juts out from the rest of the continent like a Horn. It is bordered by Ethiopia to the South, Sudan to the west and the Red Sea to the north and east. Before the Italians colonized Eritrea, it was part of the Ethiopian Empire. Eritrea and northern Ethiopia share the same languages and religions. Many of the customs are the same and historically the people were loosely united under the control of the Ethiopian Empire. Loosely united, because the Ethiopian Empire at that point in time was not a strong government and did not fully control all of the outlying areas that were included within the Emperor's possessions. Often, regional warlords or princes were more visible to the people as sources of power than the Emperor. Yet still, Eritrea was part of the highland plateau area of Eastern Africa that runs north of the Rift Valley and which was historically part of the Ethiopian Empire.

The Italians began their colonization of Eritrea through a business transaction when the Rubattino Shipping Company 'purchased' the bay and town of Assab in 1869. This was a fairly dubious beginning as the land was not purchased from the Emperor. The Italians had an eye on controlling the whole Horn of Africa, and from Assab they began to move inland, taking control of parts of modern day Somalia and attempting to take over the whole of Ethiopia. However, something unusual happened as they progressed. As the Italian army moved south from Eritrea to take over the rest of Ethiopia, they were stopped by the army of Ethiopia at the Battle of Adwa in 1886.

The Battle of Adwa

The Battle of Adwa, fought in 1896, marked the first time that a non-white nation successfully defended itself from colonial domination by a European power. At the same time, however, the outcome of the battle solidified Italy's control over Eritrea. By 1889, the Italians had been toying with a conquest of the Horn of Africa for several years. Emperor Menelik, realizing at the time that he did not have the capability to defend his entire empire

---

from the invaders,★ gave the Bogos highlands to Italy in the Treaty of Wichale; the Italians then re-named this region Eritrea. This concession, naturally, satisfied the Italians for only a short time, as they began to look toward further expansion into Ethiopia. The tension between Italy and Ethiopia finally came to a head in March of 1896 in the city of Adwa in Northern Ethiopia.

The Italians, with an army composed partly of Eritreans, entered Ethiopia in December of 1895. The Ethiopian army fought with modern rifles that had been given to them by the French. On October 26, 1896, the Italians signed the treaty of Addis Ababa, recognizing Ethiopia's independence. This was an extremely significant event for all of Africa, as it convinced many Africans and whites alike that black people were not innately inferior to whites on the battlefield. On a regional level, the separation of Eritrea from Ethiopia by the Italians set the stage for Eritrea's claim to a separate history that lead to its independence a century later.

★ The version signed by Menelik and the version signed by Italy were different, with the Italian copy acknowledging a formal cession of territory.

In 1889, the Italians formally gave up their attempt to control more territory in the Horn and declared the establishment of the colony of Eritrea. The Italian era marked the beginning of a national identity of the region of Eritrea because from this point forward Eritreans could identify a separate history from the rest of Ethiopia. However, Italian colonization lasted only about 50 years.

The defeat at Adwa was a sore point for the Italians and they harboured resentment of the Ethiopian victory for years. When they were able to rebuild their army under the fascist government of Mussolini in the 1930s, one of the first things they did, as a prelude to the Second World War, was to attack and occupy the rest of Ethiopia. The Italian occupation continued until 1941 when the British Army drove the Italians entirely from the Horn freeing Eritrea, Ethiopia and Italian Somaliland.

After the Second World War, it was unclear what would happen to Eritrea. Most of the rest of Africa at that time was still under colonial control, though independence movements were underway in many of the African countries. The newly formed United Nations was charged with the responsibility of overseeing the disposal of the former Italian colonies. The two options for the future of Eritrea that were being widely debated were independence and reunification with Ethiopia. This period was a critical juncture in Eritrean political history. Within Eritrea, it was notable for both the presence of nationalist sentiments among a limited group of Eritreans and the absence of nationalism shared by the entire territory. There was no overwhelming and united Eritrean desire for political independence. This was a result of the fact that Eritrea had been previously part of the Ethiopian Empire and Eritrean identity and experience as distinct and separate from Ethiopian identity and experience was new and not pervasive.

A desire for independence was clearly articulated by the Muslim population of Eritrea and their political party, the Independence Bloc. Muslims in Eritrea feared a future united to Ethiopia – an overtly Christian country. The Christian population, on the other hand, was inclined to favour incorporation into the Ethiopian state as they shared the same Coptic Christian religious practices and traditions. Adding to this natural affinity due to religious similarities was a threat from the patriarch of the Coptic Church in Eritrea who announced that anyone publicly supporting the independence of Eritrea would be excommunicated (Garcetti and Gruber, 2000). Thus, the discussion took on religious overtones and broke down along religious lines with the Muslims for independence and the Christians against.

FEDERATION WITH ETHIOPIA

According to research carried out by the United Nations' Four Powers Commission in charge of the dispossession of the colonies (France, UK, US and the Soviet Union) public opinion was slightly greater in favour of independence, or some sort of trusteeship that would lead to independence. Among the elites in Eritrea, a war of words was conducted between the two sides with no identifiable common ground. In 1950, the United Nations finally decided to federate Eritrea with Ethiopia. Federation was justified on the grounds that there was a great similarity in cultures between the two states and Eritrea had previously been a part of the Ethiopian empire. Federation was designed in such a way as to allow Eritrea the maximum possible autonomy within Ethiopia with safeguards in place to assure the continuity of unique Eritrean cultural and political traditions.

As the federation began, Eritrea had a great deal of autonomy and it was able to keep its unique laws – which were well-defined and mirrored those of Italy – and its two languages: Tigrinya and Arabic. Eritrea's separate identity was preserved by the fact that Eritrea was federated with Ethiopia, much in the way that Quebec is part of the Canadian federation, with guarantees of autonomy and flexibility. Eritrea had autonomy over all areas save immigration, defence and foreign affairs. However, after 1955, the Ethiopian state began a process of controlling Eritrea from the centre by eliminating the differences between Eritrea and the other Ethiopian provinces. The Eritrean flag was replaced, the Eritrean assembly was stripped of responsibility and the administration of the province was taken over by Ethiopian officials. Perhaps most disturbing to the local population was the replacement of the indigenous languages of Tigrinya and Arabic with Amharic – an Ethiopian language – as the language of instruction in the schools. The Ethiopian government began to pressure elites within Eritrea to succumb to its push for the conformity of the Eritrean province. In 1962, the Eritrean Assembly voted for full union with Ethiopia. This 'free' vote was aided by the presence of Ethiopian troops surrounding the assembly building.

This time was important in the struggle for Eritrean independence as it united Eritreans in their political desires and it gave them a common enemy – the Ethiopian state. No longer was there a clear divide among the populace with Muslims desiring independence and Christians seeking unity with Ethiopia. After 10 years of federation, few looked with favour on the future of Eritrea as a province of the Ethiopian state. By the time the Eritrean Assembly voted for union with Ethiopia, the seeds of armed rebellion were already in place.

WAR FOR INDEPENDENCE (1961–1991)

The Muslim population of Eritrea was at the forefront of the movement towards armed opposition to the Ethiopian state. Muslims were arguably the most alienated by unity with Ethiopia. The first Muslim group that emerged in the struggle for Eritrean independence was the Eritrean Liberation Front (ELF) established by Eritreans living in Egypt. In the 1970s the ELF split into factions because some ELF members wanted the organization to retain a Muslim identity and others wanted it to focus on a more secular type of nationalism that would incorporate all of the religious and ethnic groups of Eritrea. A group of younger fighters left the ELF to form what would become the Eritrean People's Liberation Front (EPLF), an armed faction that was ideologically dedicated to the equality of Christians and Muslims in the armed struggle and in a future Eritrean state.[1] The EPLF espoused a secular nationalism and emphasized Eritrean identity over ethnic and religious identities.

ELF	EPLF
Eritrean Liberation Front	Eritrean People's Liberation Front
Predominantly Muslim	All religions/all ethnicities
1960s–1981	1970s to the present day
Ethnonationalist	Secular nationalist
Exiled	Current government of Eritrea

[1] Interview with Teame Beyne, President of the High Court of Eritrea, Asmara, 1994.

Over the next 10 years Eritrean liberation groups fought each other as well as the Ethiopians and were, as a result, not very effective in achieving their objectives. However, by 1981 the EPLF managed to crush the ELF factions, driving them into exile in Sudan and Egypt. Thus, a critical ideological point was won and secular nationalism became the unifying identity among Eritreans of all ethnic groups and religions. With the defeat of the ELF, the EPLF was able to redefine ethnicity in such a way as to make 'Eritrean' not only an identity choice, but the *preferred* identity choice.

Women fighters in Eritrea

Since the 1970s, the women of Eritrea have contributed greatly to the cause of Eritrean liberation. At one time, women comprised 30 per cent of the liberation movement's fighting force, working alongside men on the battlefields of freedom. The women did not allow anything to hinder the dedication with which they fought for Eritrean independence; women who became pregnant while on military duty took maternity leaves and reported back to duty immediately thereafter. The high involvement of women in its liberation forces has led to the perception of the Eritrean People's Liberation Force (EPLF) as one of the most progressive liberation movements in the world.

Women's increased role in liberation activity has not been limited to military service but has extended to governmental and bureaucratic involvement as well. This has, in turn, allowed them to change some of Eritrea's more traditional laws regarding women. For example, consent of the bride must now be obtained before a marriage takes place, whereas previously, arranged marriages were the norm. Women are now allowed to represent themselves in court rather than being represented by a brother or father. Also, assets are now divided equally between husband and wife in case of a divorce, and daughters now have the same rights of inheritance as sons. Thus, the military involvement of women in the Eritrean liberation movement has had social repercussions in the wider Eritrean society.

Secular Eritrean nationalism with complete political and territorial autonomy was the unified goal of the Eritrean liberation movement by the late 1980s. The rhetoric of the movement, the dedication of the fighters and the growing unity of Eritreans in this goal all indicated that there was little hope for an end to the fighting until independence was achieved. Yet Ethiopia was reluctant to let Eritrea go. Many

Ethiopians considered Eritrea to be a part of their country, stolen by the Italians for a few decades and now rightfully reincorporated into Ethiopia. Added to this desire for political unity was the fact that Asmara, the capital of Eritrea, was a beautiful city that was ringed by productive factories. It was economically desirable for the Ethiopian state to maintain control of Eritrea.

THE CREATION OF ERITREAN IDENTITY

Prior to the war for the independence of Eritrea, few Eritreans actually saw themselves as Eritrean. It is not hard to imagine why this is the case. Prior to colonization, Eritrea had been loosely incorporated into the Ethiopian Empire. Many people felt a shared identity with Ethiopia, particularly the Orthodox Christian population of Eritrea. Additionally, within Eritrea there were nine different ethnic groups and many people felt a strong identification with their particular ethnic group rather than with the fighters and with Eritrean nationalism. The EPLF explicitly sought to create an Eritrean national identification for people within Eritrea throughout their struggle for independence. The principal means through which they tried to do so was the arts. The EPLF sent drama troupes across the territory they controlled to perform plays from the various ethnic groups of Eritrea and to educate the population about the nationalist struggle and the efforts of the EPLF to free *their country*. EPLF members wrote songs and poetry that was widely distributed and meant to educate the population regarding their Eritrean identity and their shared history. There was also an attempt to use the visual arts to unify and educate the Eritrean people. One example of the EPLF's use of nationalist art was a poster they issued of a large fist surrounded by nine smaller fists – a symbol of Eritrean nationalism surrounded by representations of the nine ethnic groups that exist within Eritrea. This poster is a symbolic representation of the efforts of the EPLF to unify the disparate Eritrean ethnic groups and to create a new Eritrean nationalism.

The EPLF engaged the arts in the creation of a national myth – the myth of a shared history among diverse ethnic groups with different livelihoods and different historical experiences. The use of drama, music, visual art and poetry allowed the EPLF to reach and educate an Eritrean population that spoke many languages and included many people who could not read or write.

The EPLF was incredibly effective in creating a national myth. By the time of independence, Eritrea was a country of Eritreans with a shared identity. Most Eritreans would recognize the lines of this poem by Ararat Iyob, called *An Adaptation of a Popular Song*, as capturing

135

their national experience of struggle and deprivation in the effort to gain control of the country.[2]

Flowers of pasture
Mountains and hills
Waves of happiness
While Gold springs from her generous hands
Sea ports gleam with precious stones

This was my land
Now, poverty is my crown
Forests of hope were mine by birth
Amazing light in months of sunshine
Stalks of grain bowing to the breeze
Harbours of silvery waters
Heritage of my ancestors

Beyond my bars I can see flow
The richness of my soil
My hands are bare
While my streams are full
I wonder at the destiny
That dries the water of life
Meant to fountain

The seas, the lands
Have felt our feet
Across deserts
We are spread like leaves
Cruel shadows
Have starved our bones

Endless dreams
Nights without dawn
Seeds do not kiss the earth
Weeds tie the fields. (Iyob, 1999)

This poem refers to the experiences of fighters and refugees, the tremendous strain of the struggle for independence, alongside images of hope and a strong sense of the land and its beauty. Poems like this one, repeated among the people in the evenings around the fire and in daily conversation constructed a united identity and a shared experience despite the fact that only a minority had ever shared life in the desert, the mountains and at the gleaming seaports.

This is similar to the way many Americans identify with the pioneers moving West through the 1800s and the 'purple mountains'

---

[2] My thanks to Christine Mason for indicating both the importance of poetry in the nation building process and introducing me to the poetry of Ararat.

majesty above the fruited plains' in spite of the fact that most Americans come from waves of immigration much later and most live in cities. In America, people are subscribing to an existing national myth. In Eritrea, the EPLF was *creating* a national myth.

Thirty years of war for independence gave the EPLF time to both develop and promote a national identity, as well as to bind the population together in shared experience and difficulty. War was extraordinarily effective in helping to create an Eritrean identity.

Figure 8.1 *The Sandals Memorial in Shida Square*

The Sandals memorial

Erected in commemoration of the tenth anniversary of the beginning of Eritrea's self-rule, the Sandals memorial is located in a park called Shida Square in downtown Asmara – shida being the Arabic word for 'sandal'. The memorial is unmarked and consists of two sandals made out of 20 foot sheets of metal, looking as though they have been carelessly tossed off someone's feet. The sandals are a symbol of the thirty-year-long Eritrean independence movement, which finally achieved success in 1993. This type of sandal was worn by Eritrean freedom fighters, as it was made of inexpensive plastic and was easily mass-produced. The sandal's style kept the fighters' feet cool during Eritrea's blistering summers, and the plastic straps were easily melted back together if broken. A soldier fighting for Eritrean independence was easily identifiable to the general populace by his or her sandals, so the monument remains a tribute to the fighters' struggle that needs no explanation.

SUCCESS AND FAILURE

Thirty years of war had a terrible effect on both Ethiopia and Eritrea. These two countries are very poor and money spent on the war effort was money that did not go into state development programmes or health and education needs. From the 1974 Revolution forward, Ethiopia was a Marxist state under the leadership through most of that period of Mengistu Haile Mariam. Mengistu's[3] dictatorial rule was also a brutal one and, starting in the late 1980s, Ethiopia was facing rebellion, not just from the Eritreans in the north, but from Tigrayans, another northern people, and the Oromo in the south and west of the country. When these groups joined forces in the late 1980s and early 1990s the government was forced to fight on multiple fronts and it could not win. Mengistu fled the country in 1991 when it became apparent that the days of his regime were numbered.

While the disintegration of the Ethiopian state in 1991 provided the long sought opportunity for the Eritreans to assert their independence, it was also instrumental in immiserating the population of the rest of Ethiopia due to the severe economic conditions that resulted from the diversion of state resources to the conflict. Shortages in the capital city of everything from butter to toilet paper led to a situation in which many Ethiopians, who previously thought Eritrean secession to be inconceivable, began to entertain the idea as at least the beginning of a solution to the extreme conditions of everyday life. No group at that point in time was powerful enough to force the Eritreans to stay within the state, nor was there any desire to do so. It was clear when the government fell in 1991 that whatever government might replace Mengistu was going to be ruling over a state that was geographically smaller due to the loss of Eritrea.

In July of 1991, a conference was held in Addis Ababa formally establishing the Transitional Government of Ethiopia. It was at this conference that the Ethiopian government formally recognized the right of Eritrea to hold a referendum on independence. This referendum occurred in 1993 with an overwhelming majority of Eritreans supporting a separate Eritrean state. The dream of an independent Eritrea was finally realized.

---

[3] It is customery in Ethiopia to refer to people by their first name as last names are simply the name of a person's father. Since my father's name is Daniel, I would be known as Sandra Daniel. Calling me Daniel would simply be confusing, so it is customary to use a person's first name only. Ironically, the name Mengistu in Amharic means, the government.

Issayas Afeworki

Born in 1945, Issayas Afeworki was trained as an engineer before he began fighting for the cause of Eritrean independence from Ethiopia in 1966. After joining the Eritrean Liberation Front (ELF) he took part in the formation of its break-off group, the Marxist-leaning Eritrean People's Liberation Front (EPLF). Issayas rose quickly through the ranks of the party, and had become its secretary-general by the time of Eritrean independence in 1993. On May 24, 1993, he became President of Eritrea and the leader of the young country's only political party. The following year, his party renamed itself the People's Front for Democracy and Justice.

Perceptions of Issayas' regime both at home and abroad are varied. He came to power without a democratic election and does not tolerate criticism of his regime, as witnessed by the arrest and detention of eleven dissenting former government officials in October 2001. Despite these facts, he enjoys popularity among the people of his country, who view him as a down-to-earth man. He, together with his wife and three children, live a modest lifestyle and drive the streets of Asmara in an old Toyota.

THE WAR AFTER THE WAR

Territorial separation and independence from Ethiopia had always been the goal of the Eritrean revolution. Eritrea's success led to a wave of euphoria and a determination in Eritrea to run their government differently than so many other African states that had become highly militarized and corrupt after independence. Indeed, the success of the revolution, the partition and the hopeful beginnings of Eritrean statehood led many to predict a path of peace and growing prosperity for Eritrea. A future of peaceful interaction between Ethiopia and Eritrea was assumed. However, conflict between the two countries broke out again between 1998 and 2000 over the border that divided the two states. The Boundary Commission, which had been established to draw the border in a peaceful way after Eritrean independence, collapsed. Relations between the two states began to break down in 1997 when they began to have serious economic conflicts. Disputes relating to the Eritrean change from the Ethiopian currency, the birr, to a new Eritrean currency, the nafka, led each side to demand that traded goods be paid for in a foreign currency such as dollars. This meant that goods exchanged between the two countries – and there was considerable movement of food to Eritrea and manufactured goods to Ethiopia – would become substantially more expensive in each country as they would now have to buy dollars internationally to pay for their traded goods.

The economic conflict turned violent in 1998. Conflict first broke out in the town of Badme and then extended along the length of the border. The war lasted 2 years during which time tens of thousands of soldiers and civilians were killed.

The Ethiopian–Eritrean border war was something of a surprise. The leaders of Ethiopia and Eritrea, Meles Zenawi and Issayas Afeworki, knew each other well and had collaborated in their effort to overthrow the previous Marxist Ethiopian regime. As James Paul so engagingly put it, the two leaders,

> are Tigrinya speakers whose immediate ancestors lived on both sides of the Mareb River, which now constitutes an international border determining who is an Ethiopian of Tigrayan nationality and who is a Tigrayan of Eritrean nationality. Yet once, long ago, the Mareb flowed through the heartland of the ancient kingdom of Axum which is celebrated today by many people in both countries as the cradle of their civilization. (Paul, 2000: 174)

They were raised in the same region and share similar backgrounds of working their way up in the hierarchies of their respective movements. However, their similarities did nothing to build trust between the two states. If anything, antagonism between the two leaders has escalated the conflict between the states rather than diffused it.

The war with Ethiopia was not Eritrea's only post-independence border war. Eritrea, since independence, has fought every country with which it shares a border and Yemen as well (for possession of the Hamish Islands). This intense conflict with other countries has led

some scholars to speculate that the Eritrean government *needs* to fight wars in order to unite those within the country (Tronvoll, 1999). It could also be the case that the EPLF has had difficulty making the transition from a rebel army to a government – becoming Goliath rather than David. Whatever the reason, since independence the Eritrean government has been very belligerent to its neighbours and intolerant of opposing views within the country.

THE INTERNATIONAL DIMENSION

The secession of Eritrea and its *de facto* independence was the first major change in African colonial boundaries since decolonization occurred throughout most of the African continent in the 1960s.

Since its creation in 1963, the Organization of African Unity (OAU) has had as an organizational principle the inviolability of the borders of African states. The justification for this policy was that, even though they were colonial creations, to disregard the established boundaries of African states would mean war. The OAU had a summit in 1964 addressing the issue of Eritrean secessionist efforts. At that point the desire of the Eritrean people for independence was rejected on the premise of *uti possidetis* – the legal principle of a state's right to its own territory. By 1991 it was clear that the OAU position simply didn't matter. Eritrea was going to be independent. However, it remained unclear if they would be recognized by the OAU or not. The OAU accepted the partition and independence of Eritrea and welcomed Eritrea into the organization with the justification that it, too, was a colonial creation and the conflict with Ethiopia was a remnant of colonization in the Horn.[4] Implications for this acceptance of partition as a settlement of the conflict would be felt most strongly in Sudan and Somalia, neighbours of Ethiopia that also have regional ethnic conflicts that could be cast in the same light as remnants of colonization.

Uti possidetis: 'as you now possess'

Uti possidetis is a legal doctrine stating that 'old administrative boundaries become international boundaries when a political subdivision achieves independence' (Garner, 1999). It has also been used to justify the practice whereby, at the end of an armed conflict, a country gets to retain all of the territory that it gained during the fighting. In Africa, *uti possidetis* became the unwritten standard for the establishment of borders between the newly independent nations after colonization. In order to facilitate international relations among African states, these countries simply maintained the political boundaries that had been forced upon them by the colonizing countries.

The principle of *uti possidetis* had a direct bearing on the Organization of African Unity's (OAU) refusal to recognize Eritrea as an independent country at the beginning of its movement for autonomy in the 1960s. The OAU made a practice of acknowledging statehood based on previously existing colonial borders – *uti possidetis*. So it is that, though Eritrea claimed independence from Ethiopia in 1961, the OAU refused to acknowledge this due to the fact that Eritrea had been a part of Ethiopia before the Italians colonized it. After Eritrea

---

[4] Radha Kumar (1997) in 'The Troubled History of Partition', *Foreign Affairs* 76 (1) has argued that partition has long been used as a strategy of decolonization.

declared itself independent in 1991, the OAU reversed its position and decided to recognize it as a state using the very same doctrine of *uti possidetis* that had previously been the reason for its refusal! This time, the OAU argued that Eritrea had been colonized separately from Ethiopia prior to the Second World War and thus had a separate boundary. Therefore, according to the OAU's new interpretation of Eritrea's position in light of the doctrine of *uti possidetis*, Eritrea had a right to statehood.

The change of heart on the part of the OAU was made possible by the end of the Cold War which had made the Eritrean pursuit of independence much more difficult than it might have otherwise been. Ethiopia was a superpower client and up until the Ethiopian Revolution in 1974, received a great deal of money and training from the United States. Moreover, the region of Eritrea was viewed as vital to US interests overseas as the United States established a radio relay station called Kagnew in Eritrea. After the revolution in 1974, Ethiopia switched sides and became a Soviet client state, receiving arms and training from the Eastern bloc countries. The resources, weapons and training which poured into Ethiopia as a result of the Cold War increased the wherewithal of the state in its fight against the internal Eritrean resistance movement.

It is no mere coincidence that the Soviet Union fell in 1989, and the Eritreans won the struggle for a state in the early 1990s. The communist dictatorship in Ethiopia crumbled in 1991, and as it fell, Eritrea emerged as an independent political entity. Thus, the struggle for Eritrean independence was affected by international politics as well as the domestic struggle for control.

APPLYING THE THEORIES

As in the other case studies, this chapter will end with a discussion of how the theories apply to and explain the Eritrean nationalist struggle.

Primordialism

One would think that if there was anywhere that primordialism – the theoretical school which suggests that ethnic identities are with us from birth and unchangeable – would apply, it would be in Africa where almost everyone has a very clearly defined ethnic identity. Yet it hardly seems to apply in Eritrea. It does not appear to fit this case very well because prior to the Italian occupation and establishment of a colony there was no such thing as an Eritrean identity as there was no such thing as Eritrea. The Eritrean people were not, and then they were. Their ethnic identity was created by colonization, just as their nationalist goals were created by federation with Ethiopia. The appearance of a new ethnic identity is very difficult to explain with primordialist theory. A primordialist perspective could explain why the Eritrean people would want to be reunited with Ethiopia after colonization, but not how they could form a completely new identity as a result of colonization.

Instrumentalism

During the struggle for independence, Eritrean leaders clearly sought to instil in the population an understanding of their unity and what it meant to be Eritrean. In this regard the Eritrean case fits with instrumentalist theory which suggests that leaders manipulate ethnic identities to achieve personal or communal goals. The presence of drama troupes who toured the country promoting the struggle as well as the use of art and creative writing are all indicative of an attempt to educate the population and manipulate ethnic identity. This was extraordinarily successful.

It is also certainly the case that those leading the Eritrean struggle, such as Issayas Afeworki and others, would gain a great deal of personal prestige and power should their efforts be successful. Yet, as with the case of the Catholics in Ireland, the suffering that they had to endure in order to achieve that goal was profound and the goal of independence was never assured. At any time in the struggle, it was equally likely that Issayas Afeworki would be living out his life (if he was lucky) in an Ethiopian prison, instead of becoming president of Eritrea.

Instrumentalism is helpful insofar as it explains the emergence of an ethnic identity among people who previously did not consider themselves to be Eritrean. The goals of the liberation movement and who it served separates the instrumentalist point of view from the social constructivist. Instrumentalists would suggest that independence and the nationalist agenda of Eritreans in the second half of the twentieth century benefited the Eritrean elites, those leaders with personal goals and identities tied up in the conflict.

Social Constructivism

Similar to instrumentalism, social constructivism aids in explaining the emergence of an Eritrean ethnicity. Social constructivists argue that it is political and economic circumstances combined with some ascribed (inborn) traits that form ethnic identities. Using social constructivism we need not assume that ethnic identification is manipulated to fulfill the particular agenda of a leader or an elite group. Rather, social constructivism explains the emergence of ethnic groups as a result of political and economic circumstances. Italian colonization formed a people with a distinct historical experience. After a decade of uncomfortable political unification with Ethiopia, people began to see themselves differently and eventually their political complaints led to armed rebellion. As the armed rebellion progressed more and more people began to adopt the identity of Eritrean and see their cause as aligned with the rebels rather than that of the state. Thirty years passed and we now see a new, well-defined people group with a strong sense of nationalism and a state of their own.

YOU DECIDE

What were the goals of the Eritrean liberation movements? Did the leaders stand to gain personally from success? What about the dangers they faced?
Did achieving an independent state end Eritrea's trouble with Ethiopia? Why or why not?
What might the Eritrean case teach us about other nationalist conflicts?

TIMELINE

1886   The Battle of Adwa.
1889   Italian Colony of Eritrea established.
1941   The British drive the Italians out of Eritrea.
1961   In September, the Eritrean Liberation Front (ELF) takes up arms with the purpose of freeing Eritrea from the federation government that had been established by the UN in 1952 between Ethiopia and Eritrea.
1962   On November 14, Ethiopia annexes Eritrea.
1970   The ELF divided into two groups, with the original ELF retaining its name. The Marxist breakaway group renames itself the Eritrean Peoples' Liberation Front (EPLF).
1972– The ELF and EPLF engage in civil war in Eritrea.
1974
1974   Ethiopian Emperor Haile Selassie is overthrown by the

communist-leaning military, led by Colonel Mengistu Haile Mariam.

1991 Mengistu's communist military regime collapses in Ethiopia. The EPLF establishes regional authority in Eritrea in the form of a provisional government.

1993 UN-sponsored referendum on independence in Eritrea. Eritrea becomes a sovereign state.

1998 A border war between Ethiopia and Eritrea begins.

2000 A cease-fire occurs in the border war.

2002 The border conflict is resolved when the UN announces a new border line between the two countries. The border also includes a UN-protected 'buffer zone'.

USEFUL WEBSITES

http://www.dehai.org The website of 'Eritrea Online', which provides up-to-the-minute news coverage.

http://eri24.com/news A website devoted to Eritrean news; 'impartial and objective'.

http://www.biddho.de A site devoted to everything Eritrean, from politics to sport, to opinions and chat.

http://www.netafrica.org/eritrea.htm?MSCOMTB=ICP_Country%20|%20 Eritrea Homepage of the Eritrean government, also containing information on the history and culture of the Eritrean people.

Bibliography

Garcetti, E., and Gruber, J. (2000) 'The Post-war Nation: Rethinking the Triple Transition in Eritrea', in *Regeneration of War-Torn Societies*, edited by M. Pugh. New York: St. Martins Press.

Garner, B.A., ed. (1999) *Black's Law Dictionary*. 7th edn. St. Paul, MN: West Group.

Iyob, A. (1999) *Blankets of Sand: Poems of War and Exile*. Lawrenceville, NJ: The Red Sea Press.

Kumar, R. (1997) 'The Troubled History of Partition'. *Foreign Affairs* 76 (1).

Paul, J.C.N. (2000) 'Ethnicity in Ethiopia and Eritrea', in *Autonomy and Ethnicity*, Y. Ghai ed. New York: Cambridge University Press.

Tronvoll, K. (1999) 'Borders of Violence-Boundaries of Identity: Demarcating the Eritrean Nation-State', *Ethnic and Racial Studies* 22 (6):1037–61.

Young, M.C. (1986) 'Cultural Pluralism in the Third World', in *Competitive Ethnic Relations*, edited by J. Nagel. New York: Academic Press, Inc.

CHAPTER 9

Responding to Violent Ethnic Conflict

Almost all 'ethnic' conflicts are better characterized as nationalist conflicts, because nationalism is ethnic identification that has in some way become politicized. Therefore, this chapter might just as well have been titled 'Responding to Nationalism', because by the time ethnicity leads to conflict it has developed some sort of political articulation. Bosnia, Quebec, Northern Ireland and Eritrea can all be discussed as ethnic conflicts, where the primary focus is on individual political identities, or as nationalist conflicts, where the primary focus is on the goals of the ethnic group.

All nationalisms are not violent. In some cases, such as Quebec, groups pursue their goals through the political system. Nationalisms that are peaceful in nature or which are articulated in forms that do not set them in opposition to other groups may be managed within the political institutions of a state. However, when nationalist movements pit themselves in violent opposition to other groups, as has often been the case in recent history, social scientists begin to look for solutions or accommodations to turn violence back into peaceful political participation.

Efforts to manage ethnic conflicts occur at three levels: international, national and personal. The level that is most appropriate and most effective depends on the nature of the conflict.

NATIONAL

There are two fundamental approaches that a state can have towards a group that is demanding greater rights or representation within its borders: it can accommodate those interests or it can repress them. Repression as a method of dealing with nationalist movements has not been terribly effective to date, for a state must be willing to take the most extreme measures to effectively eliminate ethnic dissent. When a state chooses the path of repression, it may fuel a nationalist conflict, rather than dampening it down.

 Crawford Young (1986) refers to the use of military intervention and one-party states to shut down the political sphere to some ethnic groups as *authoritarian containment*. He notes that the use of the coercive power of the state in this regard is not always effective and does not achieve the intended purpose. Sometimes attempts to contain ethnic expression merely add to the grievances of the group being contained. The example of Eritrea is instructive. The more the Ethiopian state clamped down on Eritrean resistance movements and attempted to control the renegade province from the centre through military strength, the more fuel was added to the fire of the Eritrean independence movement.

If coercion does not effectively quell nationalist political aspirations then what will? There are a number of possible state responses to nationalist movements that are political but non-coercive in nature. These responses run the gamut from preventative programs such as affirmative action to extreme measures such as partition.

Affirmative Action

Affirmative action is the systematic selection of individuals from historically disadvantaged groups to play a role in the government and educational systems of a country. Perhaps the best and most effective example of affirmative action policies that have addressed the concerns and historical disadvantage of a particular group are those of India. It is enshrined in the Indian Constitution that certain groups of people, referred to as the Scheduled Castes and Classes, will receive a certain number of seats in the assembly and preferential access to civil service positions and educational opportunities. The historically disadvantaged group in India specifically targeted in this endeavour is the untouchables, also known as the Dalit. The Dalit are not part of the caste system – the Hindu social and religious structure that governs the lives and social organization of most Indians. The caste system consists of five specific castes with a variety of subdivisions within them called jati. Every Hindu is part of the caste system, except the Dalit, who are completely marginalized within Indian society. The Indian system of affirmative action for certain underprivileged groups has been successful in gaining these people representation in the assembly and in the civil service. However, it is not entirely without problems as it is resented by non-Dalits. This is a typical pitfall of ethnic preference systems; they are often resented by groups that do not receive the preferences.

Federalism

Federalism, devolution or other intermediate power-sharing solutions that give some control to a particular group of people within a limited region can minimize ethnic conflict. All of the case studies in this book involve some attempt to use federalism or another type of autonomy arrangement to minimize conflict. In the case of Eritrea it was unsuccessful. In Quebec it has been successful as the Quebecers have been able to use their regional powers to construct language laws with which the majority of their population is content and protected. In both Northern Ireland and Bosnia, some sort of regional power-sharing arrangement is underway, but it remains to be seen whether these will be successful in eliminating or moderating ethnic conflicts.

The beauty of federalist arrangements lies in their flexibility. In the United States and Canada, federalism is constitutionally guaranteed. However, in other cases such as the United Kingdom and India, autonomy arrangements are contingent upon the states or regions meeting certain criteria. Thus, some sort of sub-state units can be created to meet certain representational demands and dissolved when those demands go away or when the state desires to address the problem in some other way.

Consociationalism

Originally associated with the work of Arend Lijphart (1978) consociationalism is an attempt to dissipate ethnic or national conflict through the use of bargaining and power sharing at the highest levels of the state. Lijphart discussed the role of consociationalism in European democracies, most famously, Belgium. In Belgium, there is a distinct linguistic divide between the Flemish-speaking and the French-speaking Belgian populations. Rather than allowing this ethnic difference to become mobilized into a full-blown nationalist struggle, the government of Belgium has used a variety of strategies to promote negotiation and bargaining between the two groups within the government institutions. Much of the bargaining occurs through the leaders of the two groups, who operate in a government coalition. Consociationalism has also been used in the South African Parliament and the current Northern Ireland Assembly at Stormont. Consociationalism is a political arrangement surrounded by controversy. Critics argue that it is only a superficial solution to ethnic conflict, as it continues to stress the dividing differences of ethnic groups and maintains an 'us/them' way of perceiving the situation. Others argue that it is an effective way to manage conflicts as resolution happens from the top down, rather than the bottom up.

Partition

At the far end of the spectrum of desirable political solutions to nationalist movements is partition. Partition appears to be a relatively quick and easy solution to ethnic conflicts, especially when compared to years and years of ethnic civil war. However, appearances are deceiving. Partition in both theory and practice is anything but a panacea. It is rarely the case in reality that partition actually results in two distinct homogeneous areas. If ethnic groups were divided into homogeneous areas then solutions that fall short of partition, such as federalism, might be more viable. What is more typical is that ethnic conflict and nationalist agendas arise in situations in which ethnic groups are intermingled. Or where one area which has a high population of a particular ethnic group wants to secede (such as Eritrea) and yet there are still a large number of persons from that ethnic group that will be left in the state from which partition occurs (for example Eritreans left in Ethiopia).

Additionally, problems develop when the area that wants to secede is not homogeneous either in its ethnic composition or in terms of ideology. A great example of this problem is southern Sudan. There has been a secessionist movement in southern Sudan since the 1980s. The agenda and motivations for secession are clear. The vast majority of southern Sudanese are not Muslim and yet they have been forced to live under Sharia law.

Sharia law

'Sharia' is the name for the body of Islamic law made up of the rules and regulations delineated in the authoritative Islamic texts, such as the Koran (the Islamic holy book) or Hadiths (sayings of the Prophet Muhammed). Sharia law divides all human actions into five categories: obligatory, meritorious, permissible, reprehensible and forbidden. Muslims strive to live their lives according to the Sharia law, the dictates of which strictly govern everyday behaviour. Infringements of the law can carry grave punishments, such as the amputation of limbs. Adherence to Sharia law is encouraged as a means of maintaining communal piety. Sharia law is a means of spurring fellow Muslims along in hopes of reaching the heavenly bliss described in the Koran.

Both Christians and animists in the southern area of Sudan find this intolerable and have been involved in armed conflict with the Sudanese government since the institution of Sharia law. In this case partition seems like an easy solution to the conflict. If it is the religious differences that are leading to this war, then let the Muslim north separate from the non-Muslim south and the problem will be solved. If only it were so easy. Since the 1980s there has been violent conflict in the south between various opposition armed forces. This fighting has been intermittent, but deadly. In Sudan, partition would be unlikely to put an end to ethnic violence once and for all because of the heterogeneity of the population in the south. Moreover, southern secessionist groups have often allied themselves with northern political groups that are opposed to Sharia law and sympathetic with the political aspirations of the south. These groups are unlikely to disappear if the south becomes independent.

Electoral Systems

Changing an electoral system can alter the rules of the game in a situation with entrenched and seemingly intractable ethnic conflict. This is particularly true for states that are moving from plurality or first-past-the-post voting rules to proportional representation. The 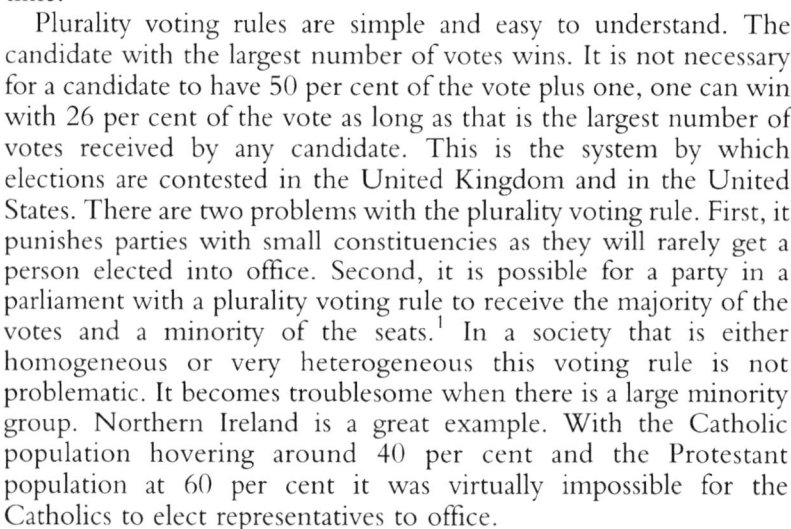 example of Northern Ireland, discussed in Chapter Six, is an excellent example of the effectiveness of changing voting rules in order to restructure political incentives. There, the switch from a plurality system to proportional representation gave Catholics the ability to have a significant voice in the political process for the first time.

Plurality voting rules are simple and easy to understand. The candidate with the largest number of votes wins. It is not necessary for a candidate to have 50 per cent of the vote plus one, one can win with 26 per cent of the vote as long as that is the largest number of votes received by any candidate. This is the system by which elections are contested in the United Kingdom and in the United States. There are two problems with the plurality voting rule. First, it punishes parties with small constituencies as they will rarely get a person elected into office. Second, it is possible for a party in a parliament with a plurality voting rule to receive the majority of the votes and a minority of the seats.[1] In a society that is either homogeneous or very heterogeneous this voting rule is not problematic. It becomes troublesome when there is a large minority group. Northern Ireland is a great example. With the Catholic population hovering around 40 per cent and the Protestant population at 60 per cent it was virtually impossible for the Catholics to elect representatives to office.

Proportional representation (PR) systems are conceptually different from plurality and majority voting rules. The idea behind proportional representation is to come up with an assembly that accurately reflects the diversity of the population at election time. The assembly should be able to reflect ethnic, ideological or religious diversity. Therefore, if 40 per cent of the population votes for Catholic parties then 40 per cent of the seats will be held by Catholic parties. If 50 per cent of the population votes for Protestant parties, then 50 per cent of the

---

[1] In fact this happened in the 1992 parliamentary election in the United Kingdom when the Conservative party won 51.6 per cent of the seats in parliament with only 42 per cent of the popular vote.

assembly should be filled with Protestant party representatives. Moreover, if the remaining 10 per cent of the vote is split between smaller parties, then these parties should also be represented in the assembly according to the proportion of the popular vote they received.

Proportional representation voting rules assure the equal weight of every citizen's opinion regardless of the number of people in his or her particular group. In this way, the assembly becomes a reflection of the electorate and major issues that are affecting the population will be heard in the assembly.

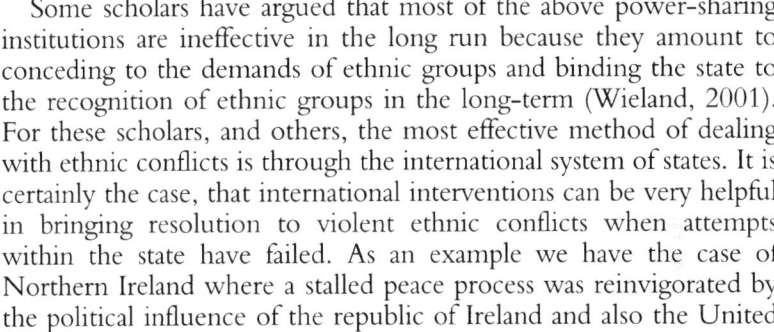

Some scholars have argued that most of the above power-sharing institutions are ineffective in the long run because they amount to conceding to the demands of ethnic groups and binding the state to the recognition of ethnic groups in the long-term (Wieland, 2001). For these scholars, and others, the most effective method of dealing with ethnic conflicts is through the international system of states. It is certainly the case, that international interventions can be very helpful in bringing resolution to violent ethnic conflicts when attempts within the state have failed. As an example we have the case of Northern Ireland where a stalled peace process was reinvigorated by the political influence of the republic of Ireland and also the United States.

INTERNATIONAL

In an increasingly globalized and interdependent world, it is not surprising that a few of the tools for responding to ethnic conflict are international. However, the choices in the international arena have been more limited, as it is often difficult to reward or penalize a side in a particular conflict if both sides are located within the same state. It is possible for international actors to get involved in ethnic conflicts on a particular side, but it is more difficult for international organizations or actors to bring about solutions to ethnic conflict.

Arms Embargoes

International interventions take a variety of forms. In cases where ethnic conflict has become violent, such as Bosnia in the early 1990s, arms embargoes can be enacted to prevent the further flow of weapons into a country. In the Bosnian case the embargo was started by the UN Security Council as a serious effort to restrict further purchases of weapons in an area where violence had begun. However, arms embargoes generally, and this one in particular, often come too late. In the case of the Bosnian War, the arms embargo meant that the

Bosnian Government forces could not purchase weapons from outside the country and this hampered their efforts in the war. The sides that armed earlier, the Serbs and the Croats, did not suffer as much as a result of the embargo. Thus, though embargoes are supposed to be blanket measures to prevent further killing, they can swing the political and strategic balance of a conflict and may not lead to a lessening of the violence.

Military Interventions

Direct military interventions are more rare than arms embargos because they are far more expensive in terms of money and lives. Three types of military interventions from outside have occurred in the past: UN peacekeeping interventions, multinational interventions such as the NATO action in the former Yugoslavia, and single-party interventions. Of these types, single-party interventions tend to be both the most controversial and the most effective – controversial because a state is typically pursuing its own goals and effective because it is able to do so in a single-minded way. For example, in the wake of the Rwandan genocide in 1994, the new Rwandan government not only stopped the genocide within Rwanda but used the genocide to justify an incursion into a neighbouring country, the Democratic Republic of Congo (DRC), for 'defensive' purposes. The Rwandan Army was able to prevent further actions in the genocide, but remained in the DRC until 2002.

UN Peacekeeping operations are another option. Peacekeeping operations are less effective because the troops are forced to adhere to their mandate, which often means not becoming involved in active defence. In both Bosnia and Rwanda, UN troops were present during violent ethnic conflict and did not prevent killing even when they were able to do so.

Military interventions and arms embargoes are solutions to ethnic conflict once it has turned violent. There is a far greater array of potential solutions to ethnic conflict at the international level before it becomes violent, or after a cease-fire has been reached.

Preventative Diplomacy

Some have encouraged preventative diplomacy by the international community to stop violent ethnic conflict before it occurs. Preventative diplomacy is a short- or medium-term intervention that occurs when violence appears to be imminent. The goal of preventative diplomacy is to prevent immediate violence and to buy time for further negotiation to develop a more lasting solution. Preventative diplomacy almost always involves some sort of mediation. By the time parties to a conflict reach a point where they are on the brink of violence, it is very difficult for them to negotiate directly. Therefore, third party mediation is needed. Third party mediation allows a person or state not directly involved in the conflict to attempt to seek an agreement between the parties to the conflict. In the cases considered in this book, there are several examples of third party mediation. In Northern Ireland, US Senator George Mitchell became a crucial mediator in the talks that brought about the Good Friday Agreement. His role and the fact that he represented US desire for a solution in Northern Ireland were critical to achieving a compromise on the key political issues. In the case of Eritrea, a solution to the border war with Ethiopia came about after intense efforts by the Organization of African Unity to push both parties to the bargaining table. In that case, the outcome was eventually determined by military action; however, the OAU was waiting to help negotiate a cease-fire and the eventual terms of peace. These are two examples of third party mediation – one successful and one less so. If we were to consider a larger set of ethnic conflicts, we would see many other examples of third party mediation aimed at achieving peace and compromise.

Ethnic conflicts are dangerous not just to a single state but to all of the surrounding states. Ethnic conflicts have the potential to spill over to other states either through the creation of refugees or by involving people of the same ethnic groups in different states. Particularly when violence is involved, spillover effects can make one country's ethnic conflict a tremendous problem for neighbouring states. The threat of spillover violence or refugee flows makes the resolution of ethnic conflicts a critical political issue not just within the country in which the conflict occurs, but also for its neighbours. In a world that is becoming more interconnected in terms of economics and politics, it is no longer the case that we can say that ethnic conflicts are a domestic issue.

PERSONAL

The real long-term solution to ethnic conflict occurs at the personal or individual level. It is only at the level of the individual that hatreds and prejudices, which lead to violence and political conflict, can be completely eliminated. However, it is extremely difficult and time-consuming to address prejudices at the individual level. In most ethnic or national conflicts that have turned violent, the critical factor needed to end the violence is some sort of mutual trust between the two sides. Without mutual trust it is virtually impossible for opposing sides to negotiate a resolution to their disputes. In 1998, Eritrea and Ethiopia went to war over their shared boundary. One of the issues that was clearly involved in the progress towards war in these countries was the profound lack of trust that had developed between the two sides as a result of the 30-year war for Eritrean independence. They had many opportunities to negotiate a settlement to their border conflict, but they could not because neither side believed the other was negotiating in good faith. The result was a war in which these two economically challenged countries spent millions of dollars and lost tens of thousands of their citizens. This is an example of how the issue of trust becomes a problem at the international level.

The problem is reflected at the individual level in every locality where ethnic conflict has become violent. Before Yugoslavia disintegrated, citizens in Bosnia lived in mixed communities of Serbs, Croats and Muslims. It is unlikely Bosnia will regain the level of trust that sort of intermixing requires in this generation or the next. The violence that occurred has left people with distrust for those of other ethnic groups because other ethnic groups have become a security threat. In these sorts of circumstances it is extremely difficult to achieve any long-term resolution to ethnic conflict. In Northern Ireland, communities are geographically divided between Protestant and Catholic. However, these clear divisions by neighbourhood did not occur until the violence began in the late 1960s and people began to see their own security as threatened by the ethnic conflict. How can these divisions brought about by personal insecurity and a lack of trust be resolved?

One of the most effective ways of addressing the lack of trust has been to work with children before they form strong ethnic prejudices. One might hope that religious groups would also be effective in helping to resolve the lack of trust between individuals of different ethnic communities. However, the evidence on this subject is mixed. Often, instead of being a source of reconciliation, religious institutions are instrumental in organizing and fomenting ethnic hatred and violence. This was certainly the case in both Rwanda and Bosnia where religious leaders and institutions facilitated the killing that occurred as a result of ethnic hatred. Scott Appleby (1999) discusses this subject at length, and his book is a good resource for those interested in the role of religion in ethnic conflicts and violence stemming from a variety of causes.

Targeting children

Some of the most effective trust-building programmes have been those that involve children. Reaching children before they develop strong prejudices or before their prejudices are reinforced by violence in conflict-ridden areas seems to be an effective way of building bridges between communities. Soccer clubs in Northern Ireland that recruit Catholic and Protestant youths to play on the same teams have introduced the children to the other community in a positive way. Similarly, preschools started in the West Bank and in Macedonia are also attempts to give children positive experiences of children from other ethnic groups and perhaps involve their parents as well. These seemingly apolitical activities can have a long-term positive benefit if at least some of the new generation can learn not to hate.

INCORPORATING THE THEORIES

What do the different theories suggest as potential solutions to ethnic conflicts?

Primordialism is perhaps the most pessimistic. If people are born with ethnic identities that never change or that are somehow biologically determined, then ethnic conflict is inevitable and simply needs to be controlled. Primordialism cannot explain why an ethnic identity would ever cease to be important. This makes it very difficult to seriously apply to considerations of nationalism because we know that certain nationalist movements disappear over time, just as some appear. If we cannot explain why some ethnic identities are more salient at different points in time or change from place to place, then the variety of conflict resolution tools one can apply is limited to autonomy or partition.

Instrumentalism is much more flexible, due to its focus on the goals and interests of the elites. Without discounting the deep-seated nature of ethnic and nationalist conflicts, instrumentalism focuses on the flexible nature of political goals. This flexibility means that the instrumentalist perspective is more hopeful regarding the possibility of resolution of nationalist conflicts. If the incentives in a conflict could be changed somehow – perhaps through the threat of international intervention or isolation – to make it less desirable for elite groups or the leaders of an ethnic group, then resolution is possible.

A social constructivist might argue that changing the economic and political grievances or incentives which led an ethnic group to become nationalist would lead them to drop their nationalist agenda. This would not be easy to achieve, but it is possible. Social constructivist approaches to resolving nationalist conflicts would focus less on elites and more on the economic and political circumstances that created the environment for nationalist conflict.

Of the three theories, instrumentalism is the most hopeful regarding solutions to ethnic conflict. Changing the incentives for a small group of people – the elites – is far easier than addressing political or economic inequality.

CONCLUSIONS

The serious political consideration of political identities and nationalist movements is new to international relations. It is not new to historians and sociologists who have long considered the waxing and waning of political identity. Political scientists, however, have for decades had tunnel vision – looking primarily at the state or at elites and not having a clear understanding of the role that individual political identities can play in politics. With the end of the Cold War and the sudden opening up of political space, many ethnic groups with nationalist agendas took the opportunity to try and gain a foothold for their cause. Thus, there appeared to be an upsurge in ethnic conflict following the Cold War. The cause of all of this 'ethnic conflict' was groups with nationalist agendas taking advantage of the new world order. What better time to try and assert the rights of your particular group then when the former bipolar world seemed to be disintegrating?

Yet these ethnic groups with political aspirations were not new. It is simply the case that the way that we think of them politically has changed over time. The absence of many groups challenging their states or demanding rights during the Cold War was a result of the fact that any threat to a US client state would be treated as a threat to US interests. The same was true for the Soviets and their client states. The Cold War was therefore not a congenial time for nationalist movements. Now, nationalist movements may not be viewed favourably by their states or outside countries, but they are unlikely to be labelled ideologically as communist or capitalist and therefore seen as a threat on a more universal scale.

Political identities are exceedingly important to both state and international politics in the long-run. States need to be able to manipulate political identities within their borders and manage nationalist movements once they develop. Good states will fulfil both these requirements in a positive and peaceful manner, encouraging individuals to choose benign political identities or those that support the state. Internationally, we have witnessed the effect that ethnic conflicts have on neighbouring states in the Great Lakes Region of Africa, in the Indian subcontinent and in the Balkans. Ethnic conflict is of international concern because it is an international security issue.

Incorporating nationalism and political identity into our analysis of state and international politics leads to a more accurate, though perhaps more complicated, way of understanding the world and the political actions of those in it. The ethnic and political identities that individuals carry are as important as their ideological beliefs. These identities cause people to make political decisions that we cannot comprehend without understanding why people carry particular ethnic identities and how they become politicized.

Bibliography

Appleby, R. S. (1999) *The Ambivalence of the Sacred*. New York: Rowman & Littlefield Publishing.

Wieland, C. (2001) '"Ethnic Conflict" Undressed', *Nationalities Papers* 29 (2):207–41.

Young, M. C. (1986) 'Cultural Pluralism in the Third World', in *Competitive Ethnic Relations*, edited by J. Nagel. New York: Academic Press, Inc.

INDEX

Printed in Great Britain
by Amazon.co.uk, Ltd.,
Marston Gate.